T0392291

AUTOBIOGRAPHY OF AN OLD SCHOOL SOUTH AFRICAN SON

PETER BOSHOFF

© 2022 Peter Boshoff. All rights reserved.

No part of this book may be reproduced, stored in a retrieval system, or transmitted by any means without the written permission of the author.

AuthorHouse™ UK
1663 Liberty Drive
Bloomington, IN 47403 USA
www.authorhouse.co.uk
UK TFN: 0800 0148641 (Toll Free inside the UK)
UK Local: 02036 956322 (+44 20 3695 6322 from outside the UK)

Because of the dynamic nature of the Internet, any web addresses or links contained in this book may have changed since publication and may no longer be valid. The views expressed in this work are solely those of the author and do not necessarily reflect the views of the publisher, and the publisher hereby disclaims any responsibility for them.

Any people depicted in stock imagery provided by Getty Images are models, and such images are being used for illustrative purposes only.
Certain stock imagery © Getty Images.

Front cover photo by PAW Photography.

This book is printed on acid-free paper.

ISBN: 978-1-6655-9638-1 (sc)
ISBN: 978-1-6655-9637-4 (e)

Print information available on the last page.

Published by AuthorHouse 02/14/2022

CONTENTS

ABOUT THE AUTHOR

Peter Boshoff was born at the end of the second World War,

The eldest of 6 brothers.

He was single for 25 years, married to his first wife for 25 years and married to his second wife for the last 25 years.

He led a full and interesting life and is intrigued in everything around him and is constantly looking to widen his horizons.

Most of what he knows about life is due to his own experiences and avid reading. More than half of his books are technical or classical literature, apart from all his medical books and can fill a small library.

Read about the history of his four grandparents and his life in this book.

He is now retired and loves writing.

Watch this space for more publications.

OTHER BOOKS BY THE SAME AUTHOR

World WARI Diary of Private Brooks on the Western Front.

ISBN 978-0-9576489-0-6 In paperback at Amazon.com

ISBN 978-0-9576489-1-3 in e book Kindle at Amazon.com

ISBN 978-0-9576489-2-0 e book Pdf

Published 2013

Het Concentratie Kamp van Irene: Transcribed from original Dutch to Digital Format and translated into English and Afrikaans.

ISBN 978-0-9576489-3-7 … … In paperback at Amazon.com

Het Concentratie Kamp van Irene 2nd Edition: Transcribed into digital format in Dutch, and translated into English and Afrikaans.

ISBN 978-0-9576489-4-4 … … in paperback at Amazon.com

Published 2016

Autobiography of an Old School South African Son. PETER BOSHOFF.

1943 – 2028?

My life in a bygone era – which is almost forgotten by the younger generation, who mostly live for themselves and are not interested in the life of anyone else, except their own.

"In every old person there is a young person that asks – What the hell went wrong!"

This biography text is subject to copyright and represent the lives of real people, mostly dead by now. Any link to living people today is down to family ties and is due to their ancestors.

I do not claim copyright over any of the photos and thereby don't deny anyone else using copies of the photos. In South Africa most people are part of one whole big family and they are free to copy any of the photos, but the text is my own and part of my intellectual property and subject to copyright.

Published in paperback and ebook.

FOREWORD

This autobiography is supposed to tell the story of my own life and that of my ancestors, as no-one came about without ancestors. As I have done some genealogical research, I came to realise quite a long time ago, that I am not only a Boshoff, but also a Badenhorst, Joubert and Pretorius. (My grandparents and all their female ancestors). Genealogy is like a patchwork quilt stitched together, by copulation.

With quite a number of old photos, many of which are older than one hundred years, I would like to leave this behind to those that follow me or for those who just like to read biography's.

My story overlaps with a lot of other people, who are closely related, or further apart. It just as well could have been written by many of my contemporaries who may be closely related or further apart, provided that they have told their stories. I was often put to bed by my contemporaries, but by telling my story, it is now my chance to have the last word.

Culture is much more than just history – it is quotes and folklore and sometimes family jokes. It is about how you think and communicate as part of a group. I am proud of my Afrikaner culture, although I have changed a lot with time and taken on other values, which proves that culture isn't stagnant, but growing all the time and as within a nation. Everything is not black or white, there are a lot of shades of grey in between. Everything is not holy and holy truth can often be taken with a pinch of salt.

As a child I'd been conscious of my own sense of justice. Often people said I should become an advocate. I struggled with the concept that a guilty party could be proven to be "innocent".

(Until I learned that it wasn't the truth. It had to do with proving someone was guilty, without a doubt. You had to point out anything that could be questioned). Often people become so convinced of their points of view, which are based on sentiment rather than facts or evidence.

This also broaches on political correctness, which I resist vehemently as it doesn't always reflect the truth. The context can change by argument giving it a complete different colour. The original narration is in context with the time and the honourability of the origin is equally important. It gives meaning to the purpose in my life, which is to retain perspective and my right to form my own opinion.

Numerous events in the past have been proven to be incorrect, but that doesn't make my ancestors liars – they simply did not have all the facts and insights. When you read the old narrations, you can understand why the old folk acted as they did and you can understand why they did so. Everything needs to be judged on this basis. By writing off everything as wrong one hundred years later, without knowing the background and events of the time, you would be just as wrong. (If the ancestors had the weapon and wisdom of retrospection of the present day at their time, they might have acted differently) They were mostly farmers and a lot of Nation and church leaders simply bulldozed them and they became followers, without thinking for themselves. I would rather believe what my grandmother told me about what her grandmother told her of what happened in 1840, than I would believe a writer, who had no first or second-hand accounts of what happened. My grandmother had a first-hand account from her grandmother, who witnessed herself what had happened in those times.

Albeit, norms have changed from the time where numerous cousin marriages took place, due to lack of opportunity to meet people outside small communities. In some instances, it has even been the preference to marry cousins to keep undesired matches out of the bloodline. The latter argument was however an excuse for incest and was kept highly secret as the shame of it was so great. It doesn't mean that it did not take place. In some of the Pretorius lines inbreeding was quite common, so much so that children were born with 12 fingers or toes and was referred to as a Pretorius trait. In my own family lines 10% of my ancestors have been Pretorius and I was born with 12 fingers.

Words of Afrikaans, Dutch and native origin has been retained as it was. A lot of the place names are not able to be translated to English. Some surnames have dual spellings.

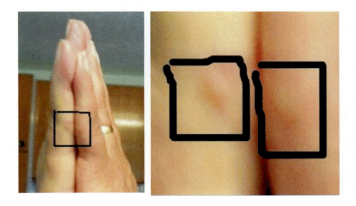

The extra fingers were only pedunculated outgrowths and when I was born the outgrowths were twisted around each other. Until the doctors tied off the outgrowths my hands were joined together.

HONOUR TO MY BOSHOFF ANCESTORS

Everyone has 2 parents, 4 grandparents, 8 great grandparents, 16 2xgreat grandparents, 32 3xgreat grandparents, 64 4xgreat grandparents and 128 5x great grandparents. I know who **all** of my ancestors are, by researching the family histories. I will only discuss my four mainlines.

Before I start with my autobiography itself, I would like to explain from where my own people came:

My **5x great grandfather** Willem Hendrik Boshoff, born c. 1720 and married 15/10/1752 to Martha Maria Cordier, was the first Boshoff that arrived in South Africa. He was the Boshoff progenitor and was a locksmith and a portside gunner. I owe my Boshoff surname to him. He departed on 27/10/1740, from Texel in the ship, Ruijven, under Captain Bernardus Heymans. (63 passenger died and 28 became very ill during the journey to the Cape.) The Ruijven arrived in the Cape on 18/3/1741. Willem and several others had been too ill to continue with the onward journey to Batavia. Willem had scurvy and with a normal diet of the time it took several months to recuperate, as the treatment was not goal orientated. He made good use of his illness to remain in the Cape. Immigrants were appointed by contract to the HOIK (Dutch East Indian Company) or had to be religious refugees.

He asked for his attestate from Altona (Bayonne). The postal service took anywhere from one and a half to two years for the return journey by sea. When the attestate finally arrived it was in French and he could not use it, but it remained in family possession. It created the postulation by some of his descendants that he was of French origin. He did however in the interim proved his worth in the Cape and he was accepted in service of the Dutch East Indian Company. (HOIK)

The Boshoff progenitor eventually had 8 sons and 2 daughters. (Later research showed there was another illegitimate half-brother and half-sister with Cornelia Cockzaaya, a slave, but this was not included in his genealogy.)

I stem from the Boshoff progenitor's eldest son, Willem Hendrik Boshoff b1, born 1754 married to Lea Barnard, my **4x great grandparents**. (In the South African genealogy the progenitors are the first person of each surname that arrived in South Africa and were allotted the postfix "a1" and if more than 1 of the same surname "a2" etc. Their children were allotted "b1, b2" etc." Their children then became a1b1**c1**, **c2**, **c3** etc.)

I stem from this Willem Hendrik Boshoff b1's third child, namely Willem Hendrik Boshoff a1b1c3 (the 3rd child of the 1st child of the progenitor), born 7/4/1783 who married to Christina Catharina de Jager, my **3x great grandparents**. Thus 3 Willem Hendrik Boshoffs in succession. There were numerous Willem Hendrik Boshoff cousins and nephews and that is where the notations becomes very helpful.

Willem Hendrik Boshoff's (a1b1c3) 10th child **Hans Jurgen Boshoff a1b1c3d10**, born 1816 and married to Martha Maria Catharina Fourie,(my **great great grandparents).** They had 4 children.

He was later married to Geertruida Elizabeth Lambrecht and had a further 3 children with her. He died 26/7/1886.

Hans Jurgen Boshoff's 3rd child, **Willem Hendrik Boshoff a1b1c3d10e3**, born 1843, with his first wife, Martha Fourie, was my **great grandfather.**

Willem Hendrik Boshoff a1b1c3d10e3's first wife was Lea Magdalena Boshoff, his first cousin, with whom he had 8 children. His second wife was Helena Maria Catharina Germishuyzen and he had another 8 children with her.

I stem from Willem Hendik Boshoff b1c3d10e3 and his **second wife**, Helena M C Germishuyzen, my **great grandparents**. Their 3rd child was Petrus Johannes Daniël Boshoff, my **grandfather**. (the 11th child of Willem Hendrik Boshoff b1c3d10e3.) My grandfather was named after his 2nd wife's father, Petrus Johannes Daniël Germishuyzen.

Petrus Johannes Daniël Boshoff, born 1885 was married to my grandmother Anna Johanna Magrietha Badenhorst and had 10 children. My **father** was the 8th child and named Petrus Johannes Daniël Boshoff, born 22/4/1919 and married on 8/1/1943 to my **mother**, Rachel Jacoba Joubert, born 1/8/1922.

I was their eldest child, born 3/12/1943, named Petrus Johannes Daniël Boshoff, one of six sons.

My 3rd child was also named Petrus Johannes Daniël Boshoff, born 9/8/1982, who might not have been mine.

Having in mind to prove my genealogy and more recent events, I have done my Y-DNA, my Autosomal or Family Finder DNA and my mt-DNA. Y-DNA is measured in genetic distances "0" for Recent matches (Recent in genetic terms means in the last 1,000 years and "4" signifies 4 mutations and thus multiple thousands of years ago.

Parts of the Y-chromosomes you have, determines which Y-haplo group you belong to. Which when interpreted together with genealogy and the most recent common ancestor is where the individuals meets up with each other. If both individuals have done a Family finder test and they match, you can actually see what part of the somatic chromosomes are in common to both. (MRCA)

I had a close Y-DNA match with a Boshoff that lives in the Netherlands who had done a Y-DNA12 test, which is a very basic test and not very specific. With referring to his genealogical tree he was a Boshoff a1b1c3d10e4 descendant, Boshoff a1b1c3d10e4 was a brother of my great grandfather. The Most Recent Common Ancestor was thus Hans Jurgen Boshoff b1c3d10, my great great grandfather. Both Haplogroup R-M259. This proves that in the genealogical tree after Hans Jurgen to this Boshoff and also to myself there has been no visitors to the females in this instance.

I then paid for another Netherland Boshoff, who's uncle had been in contact with the South African genealogists, Kallie Heese and this Netherland Boshoff was also a R-M259 haplogroup, but with 16 mutations between us – thus very distant and beyond genealogical reach.

I am now waiting for a closer match with another Netherland participant and also for a more distant cousin in South Africa, who will have the South African progenitor as a MRCA.

One of my brothers believed he was not my father's son and he did his Y-DNA and also his Family Finder DNA and to his dismay he was a close match to myself with "0" distance and the same haplogroup. With Family Finder he had 2600 centimorgan in common with me, as you would expect with full siblings. Children would have ½ that number and first cousins a quarter.

A descendant of my grandfather's brother was adopted and he had 1/8th of 3000 centimorgan in common with me and we have been able to determine our MRCA, who was my great grandfather, Willem Hendrik Boshoff b1c3d10e3. This proves what a great tool genetic testing can be.

The Dutch themselves had their borders shifted several times in history and in different times they mixed with German and French people. People have also moved around over the years and German and French people has moved into the Netherlands and vice versa. Neither the Dutch, Germans and French are made up of just one nationality and the composition of the population under discussion depends on the specific time era.

Further back in 1655 with the 3rd year commemoration of the Cape and the arrival of van Jan van Riebeeck, a Ds. Hermannus Bushoff, (both him and Jan van Riebeeck were from Culemborg,

Netherlands) delivered a sermon, before Hermannus journeyed to <u>Batavia.</u> So there were likely other Boshoff descendants in Batavia, which was why Willem Hendrik might have wanted to go there.

In this time period according to the Dutch archives, five other Boshoffs went to Batavia, who might have been relations to Willem Hendrik Boshoff, the South African progenitor. In the same period unrest was stirring in Batavia and with relatives there he might have become aware of it, hence his fight to remain in the Cape. A Chinese slaughter occurred 7 - 12 October 1740, preceded by a period of unrest.

The earliest Boshoffs in Netherlands has been the Coldenhoven Boshoffs of 1375 AD, who were in service of the van Gelres. As a religious family their genealogy was retained, but with large gaps. All the Boshoffs in Netherlands and South Africa might have had their origins from them. The problem is that with just one or two generations missing, the narration loses its thread.

Hans Jurgen Boshoff *1816.

with Geertruida Elizabeth Lamprecht, his 2nd wife . His 2nd marriage. She was
30 years old and was in Colesberg, when he was 34 years old.

I stem from his 1st marriage with Martha Maria Fourie, (no photo) and their 3rd child, Willem Hendrik
Boshoff b1c3d10e3, born 8 July 1843 in George, thus 100 years before myself. (My great grandparents).

Willem Hendrik b1c3d10e3 at 23, 45 and 65 yr of age. Willem b1c3d10e3's first wife (4th photo)
was his first cousin, Lea Boshoff b1c3d9e5, born 1846 and he had 8 children with her, and
another 8 children with Helena Maria Catharina Germishuizen, born 1863 on last photo.

Helena was 20 years younger than Willem Hendrik. He married Helena in 1881 when she was 18
and he was 38 years old. The Boshoffs from whom I descend were follow on pioneers and not
part of the "big trek". Helena's younger sister, Johanna Petronella, born 1876, 13 years younger

than Helena and 5 years old at her sister, Helena's wedding, later married Willem Daniël Boshoff, one of Willem Hendrik's sons with his cousin, Lea Boshoff.

Willem Daniël was 3 years old at his father's 2nd marriage. When he was 17 and Johanna 19 years old in 1895, the two of them married. (He married his stepmother's sister) They knew each other for 14 years before they married. Their 4th son was also named after Petrus Johannes Daniël Germishhuyzen. This Petrus Johannes Daniël Boshoff was born 1903.

Willem Hendrik Boshoff e3, later farmed at Tweespruit in OVS. He ended up as a farmer's foreman, but was allowed to be buried on the farm. Usually only the owners were buried on the farm. It was close to Philippolis, where my grandfather was born.

Hans Jurgen Boshoff and his family 1866 with the wedding of his daughter, in Fauresburg.

Hans Jurgen was born in George and he moved to Fauresburg after his marriage to Geertruida Lambrecht in 1846. (Until he had his 4th child he stayed in Vaalbank, close to Colesberg.)

On the photo, my great greatgrandfather Hans Jurgen, d10. Also e3(Left front) and his 1st wife, Lea Boshoff b1c3d9e5, his first cousin and all his brothers and sisters with their partners.

e1, Anna Aletta, his sister was married to Daniël Joubert, marked "5", who was related to my grandfather Joubert's ancestors. His cousin's daughter, Magdalena Martha Cornelia Joubert b5c7d2e7f2 was married to my mother's father's grandfather, Jan Abraham Joubert b9c8d9e7.

e2, Christina Catharina, the 2nd daughter, married to her first cousin, Adam Boshoff (b1c3d1e5), marked "6", the 5th child of Hans Jurgen's eldest brother; (Thus 2 first cousin marriages in the family).

e4, Louis Petrus Johannes Marthinus Boshoff, the youngest brother of e3, married to Johanna Christina Cecilia Claassens, marked "3". He was a POW in Ceylon.

e5, top left, Johannes Juergen, e3's half brother, the eldest son van Geertruida Lamprecht and

e7 the youngest son, Christoffel Hendrik, e3's youngest half brother.)

The photo was taken at the wedding of Hans Jurgen d10's 2nd youngest child, Aletta Catharina, marked e6, with Johannes Petrus Roux, marked "4" (Willem Hendrik e3s youngest half sister) in 1866.

There were four children with Martha Maria Catharina Fourie and three chidren with Geertruida Elizabeth Lamprecht, marked "1".

(No. 2 likely the father of Johannes Roux, the bridegroom.)

I have contacted some of the children's descendants on the photo. The exceptions being e2, e6 and e7. Also with the **descendant** of e3f3, the half-brother of my grandfather.

Louis Willem Boshoff e5f6 was married to Lily Rautenbach, who was shot by an English soldier and her grandson married the granddaughter of the soldier who shot her. They discovered this after genealogical research.

I am friends with their daughter.

Quite a few my relatives were involved in the Anglo Boer war of 1898 and I lost some of them in the British Concentration camps, both in my Boshoff line and in my maternal grandmother's line, Rachel Jacoba Pretorius.

I have also become friends with other descendants of the progenitor.

I have also met with several family members on the Badenhorst and Pretorius family on public media.

I also contacted almost all my maternal grandmother's sibling's descendants as well as my own cousins and their children, mainly on Facebook. (I have known my maternal grandmother's youngest sister.) My father's youngest sister, Rita had a funeral letter of my grandfather's eldest sister. (The eldest child of my great grandfather and Helena Germishuyzen) that was in a bible, gifted by P J D Germishuyzen to Helena. This related to the funeral of Martha Susanna Boshoff on 10/10/1894. She died at 12 years, 1 month and 25 days of age. Died of unknown cause after a period of illness.

The pall bearers were:

Willem Boshoff the younger. (Likely Willem Hendrik e3)
Jurie Germishuys – Family in law to Willem Hendrik.

Hendrik Horn

Andries Swanepoel.

Other people who were thanked for their contribution of the funeral arrangements were:

Willem Boshoff

Petrus Boshoff

Petrus Germishuyzen the elder – Father in law of Willem Hendrik e3.

Daniël Blignaut the younger

Christiaan Pieterse

Hendrik Pieterse

John Dippenaar

Hans Pretorius

Cornelius Gouws

Piet Steyn

Jogchem Mentz

Piet Mentz

Jan van Eeden

Theunis Kruger

Willem van den Berg.

The fact that the bible was gifted to Helena Germishuys by her father P J D Germishuyzen proved the relationship between them.

(In a Germishuyzen family webpage no mention is made of Helena Maria, but only of her sister Johanna Petronella. I've not been able to find a death notice of P J D Germishuyzen.)

GENETICS.

The human body's cells have 46 chromosomes, 22 pairs of autosomal chromosomes with an X and Y sex chromosome in males and 2 times X chromosomes in females.

Y-DNA testing is the analysis of the Y chromosome only and consists of haplogroups assigned to a genetic haplo group tree with letters of the alphabet.

In my part of the haplo group tree is assigned to the letter "R". As mutations take place you move to different parts of the tree. (Mutations take place in the order of once every 1,000 to once every 50 years, depending on what part of the chromosome is tested.)

The classification is based on the sequence of the nucleic acids with patterns and places on each chromosome. Thus abc 1, 2 and 3. The Capital letters represent the main classification. The short form is represented with coded symbols e.g., R-M269, R-L51 etc. This can be represented in a haplo group tree in order of mutations.

The deeper the level of testing, the more narrowed down the results become. As you move into the finer branches the lesser the number of surnames that appear in each branch until eventually it comes down to certain individuals of each tree and finer branches.

The more sophisticated test is the big Y testing that differentiate and separate surnames and individuals.

The male Boshoff's with ascending levels of testing are Y-DNA R-1b1a2a1a1bc3 or R-M269, R-L51, R-U152, R-L2, R-L20 and ultimately R-CTS9733 and R-BY3554 with additional terminal SNP testing. Branches, sub-branches and fine branches of the haplo group tree.

The genetics can then be combined with genealogy and provide proof of certain bloodlines. Anomalies can arise due to non-paternal events, non-disclosed adoptions, adultery and incest, but also due to quirks of genetics.

On Autosomal DNA level, where all chromosomes are compared, you get a much wider comparison and in combination with genealogy and determining the MRCA (Most recent common ancestor) you can determine relationships with unknown people. Autosomal DNA is measured in centimorgans with 2,000 to 3,000 between siblings and twins, approximately 1500 between parents and children. (If the parents are related it can be higher,) Cousins approximately 750. It halves with each generation further apart. With distant relatives in the South Africans, where you may be related in more than one way, you end up with 25 to 50 centimorgan where the progenitor is 200- to 300 years in the past. Most South Africans with forebears going back to 1650 to 1700 are related in this way due to the closed and limited gene pool.

With mt-DNA (mitochondrial DNA - Nothing to do with X chromosomes). This is contained in the nucleolus in each cell and is a cyclic chromosome carried over to the next generation but only females can pass it on to their offspring. Thus, you can build up a matriarchical family tree. Mother's mother's mother etc.

This is also measured in genetic distance in terms of mutations apart and you have a separate mitochondrial haplo group tree with also a migratory route according to origin, as you get with the Y-DNA.

A word of warning that the letters used in the mt-DNA haplogroup tree coincide with letters Used in Y-DNA haplo group tree, so you always must specify if it is a Y or mt-haplo group.

THE BOSHOFFS IN PHOTO'S

Portrait of Hans Jurgen Boshoff b1c3d10. My great great grandfather, born 1816.

Portrait of Willem Hendrik b1c3d10e3 My great grandfather, born 1843.

My grandfather, Petrus Johannes Daniël Boshoff, *1885.

and my grandmother, Anna Johanna Margaretha Badenhorst * 1886.

(My grandfather was Boshoff b1c3d10e3f11 and my grandmother
was Badenhorst b2c5d6e3f5g5, one of twins.)

One of my grandfather's half-brothers, Christoffel Hendrik Boshoff *c.1878. His mother was Lea Boshoff, W.H. Boshoff e3's first cousin and wife. (e3 = My Great grandfather)

Louis Johannes Albertus, a younger brother of my grandfather, born 1892 With his wife, Hester Maria Beukes, born c. 1900.

Elizabeth Louisa Wilhelmina Boshoff, the 2ⁿᵈ youngest sister of my grandfather. She was born 1896.

Louis Johannes Albertus born 1892 was one of my grandfather's younger brothers. (A son of Louis Boshoff and Hester Maria Beukes, born c. 1900 as an illegitimate child, who had been adopted by the Swart family. The adopted child did a Y-DNA and I met him on FB and exchanged information.)

I don't remember any of my grandfather's siblings and I don't think I have ever met any of them, but my father did. I have frequently heard of a Jurie, a brother younger than my grandfather. He farmed on Erna, just outside Fochville close to Potchefstroom. There was a sister, Helena Maria, between him and my grandfather.

I can remember that my grandfather could rattle off the names of all his half and full siblings. Luckily, they are all recorded in a Boshoff family book. (3ʳᵈ Edition.)

I know who everyone is in the photos in my possession, but my descendants won't ever know unless I publish them combined with their names - Mad about old photos, especially if you know who they are and you know where they fit in.

What I know about my grandfather, myself, is that he never talked much and only volunteered information if he was questioned. He was often away from home with his work, as a school building inspector. He also wandered off on his own, but always returned home. He also was a locust official and he wasn't present at my father's wedding.

What intrigued me was that my father always addressed his father as "Uncle Kobie" and his mother as "aunt Grietjie". They visited our small holding in Brentwood Park and that was the last time I saw them together.

My grandfather had an old Ford Consul.

My Father PJD Boshoff*1919,

My Mother before and on her wedding day. Born 1/8/1922. At that time there were no coloured photos, but my father coloured her photos in with printers pigments.

Burt Joubert, My Father, My Mother, Stella Wolmarans, Unknown flower girl in front.

Rear L to R: My Father's mother Magrietha Badenhorst * Burt Joubert * 1921, (My mother's cousin) My mother's parents, Rachel Jacoba Pretorius and Daniël Pieter Joubert. Only my father's mother was at the wedding. His father was absent.

THE BADENHORSTS
AND VERMEULENS

Claasina Frederika Cecilia Grabe, born 1842, Johannes Urbanus Vermeulen's 3rd wife.

My Father's mother's grandmother or my father's great grandmother. She was 18 years and Johannes Urbanus 45 years old, when they married. She was in Johannes Urbanus's Religious instruction school. My great great grandmother on my father's mother's side. She had 11 children.

Her eldest daughter, Martha Susanna Vermeulen married Philippus Cornelius Badenhorst. (My great grandparents on my father's mother's side).

Claasina was one year younger than Johannes Urbanus's eldest child. Claasina was stepmother to 8 children and had 11 children with Johannes Urbanus. She was the 3rd wife of Johannes Urbanus Vermeulen. After the death of Johannes Urbanus, Claasina remarried and had a further

2 children and she knew she was the mother. I traced the ancestors of both Johannes Urbanus Vermeulen and Claasina Frederika Grabe up to their progenitors.

By doing a mitochondrial DNA on my father's sister's daughter I determined that my grandmother was Mitochondrial haplogroup U-4c1 and the pure female line line led to Anne Souchay, born 1655.

ANNE SOUCHA With her as MRCA and the descendants of 2 of her daughters :

Anne Fouche b3 x Pierre Jourdan Progenitor	Susanna Fouche b7 X Louis Le Riche Stamvader
Susanna Jourdan X Jan Jordaan (Not son of Pierre.)	Susanna Le Riche b1 X Louis Fourie b6
Elisabeth Jordaan X Andreas Nolte (Progenitor)	Francina Fourie b6c5 X Jan Andries Holtshauzen b3
Anna Susanna Nolte X Lourens Rasmus Erasmus b3c4d4	Susanna Elisabeth Holtshauzen 1759 X Jacobus Steyn b1c6d2
Maria Magdalena Erasmus 1798 |Susanna Elisabeth Steyn 1783 X Jan Gijsbert du Plessis b1c9d12	
X Jacobus Johannes Petrus Erasmus	
Johanna Elisabeth Erasmus X Pieter Willem Antonie Roux	Martha Susanna du Plessis 1807 b1c9d12e1 X Jan Fred Gotl Greeve
Anna Susanna Roux X George Diederick Engelbrecht d4e2	Claasina Fredrika Grabe 1842 X Johannes Urbanus Vermeulen
Aletta Catharina Joh Elis Engelbrecht Martha Susanna Vermeulen X Philippus Cornelius Badenhorst	
X Johannes Lodewyk Pieterse|	
Aletta Catharina Joh Elis Pieterse	Anna Johanna Margaretha Badenhorst X PJD Boshoff
X Johan Ernest van Staden	

One of their daughters is mtDNA U-4c1 haplogroup Her granddaughter, my female cousin is mtDNA = U-4c1

NB: This confirms that with my assumed identities mentioned above, that there is a **genealogical** and **genetic match** with Anne Souchay as MRCA.

This proved that my father's matrilinear line was correct. I was forced to work in the dark due to family wanting to remain anonymous and the infernal laws on privacy, but I got there in the end with the help of google and geni.

Anne Souchay and all her daughters and their daughter's daughters, etc, up to my cousin will all be mt-Haplogroup U-4c1 and any new links will further confirm my father's matrilinear line – present time to the past and back to the present time.

Johannes Urbanus Vermeulen, born 1815. b1c2d3e4f4. Man of the church
with 19 children, and he was happy they were all his.

He was instructed by the church leaders in Colesburg to found a town on the Orange river, named "Hopetown", in 1854. He obtained a farm for himself, called Elandsdraai, where he remained until his death. He was married at age 25 with a bride of 24, age 38 with a bride of 20 and at 45 with a bride of 18. (A younger bride with each successive marriage), and the waiting period between marriages got shorter, only 6 months before his 2nd marriage and only 3 months before his 3rd marriage.

Johannes Urbanus was 25 years old at his 1st marriage to Christina Susanna Helena Badenhorst who was 24 years old at the time. He had five children with her – all of them daughters.

At 38 years of age, 6 months after his first wife's death, he married his 2nd wife, Hendrieka Fourie, 20 years old and had 3 children with her.

Within 3 months after the death of Hendrieka, he married 18 years old Claasina Frederika Grabe when he was 45 years old. Thus almost been 3 x her age. She was in his religious instruction class. He had 11 children with her. Johannes Urbanus produced 19 children in total, if they were all his own.

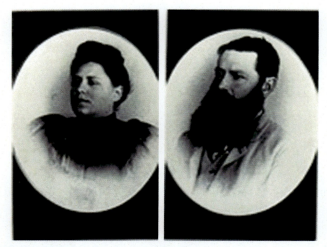

Claasina, born 1870, the 2nd youngest child of Claasina, born 1842, with her husband, Wessel Jacobus Badenhorst. My grandmother Badenhorst's aunt and her husband. This Claasina was the sister of Martha Susanna Vermeulen, my maternal grandmother's mother.

Philippus Cornelius Badenhorst *1858, Married to Martha Susanna Vermeulen, *1861 in
Hopetown, the parents of my grandmother, Anna Johanna Margaretha Badenhorst, *1886

Philippus Cornelius Badenhorst was married for a 2nd time in 1897 to Heiltjie Johanna Steenkamp, so my grandmother had 3 half sisters and one half brother. My Father knew them all, as well as my grandmother's twin sister (Aunty Klasie)*1886

Johannes Urbanus Vermeulen's great great great grandfather, the Vermeulen progenitor was married to an Indian slave, Catharina Opklim circa 1684. Ironically my Father's nickname 230 years later was Piet-Coolie and my Father's brother was Bap-Coolie as they both tanned a deep brown under the sun. My grandmother Badenhorst herself had quite frizzy hair. (Short curls that were straightened with effort.)

Anna Johanna Margaretha   Heilie *1898   Mali *1900

Issie * 1902   Johan*1904   ClaasinaFrederika

My grandmother Badenhorst * 1886 with her half-sisters and half-brother (the last photo her twin sister). My father knew them all and I remember him talking about them – he also knew Tannie Klasie, my grandmother's twin and talked about her. Last photo.

Years later I myself courted Johan's daughter, when she studied at the Pretoria Education College. She once visited me in Durban North, years after I had married. I named my first car after her. It was very difficult to hold the car in the road due to the play in its steering mechanism.

On occasions my parents and family visited some of these Badenhorsts on their orange tree farm, close to the Kruger Park's Mallelaan gate. (My adopted son's biological grandmother was also a Vermeulen, but in this case it led to The Vermeulen progenitor's brother, who was married to Maria from Bengale from India.)

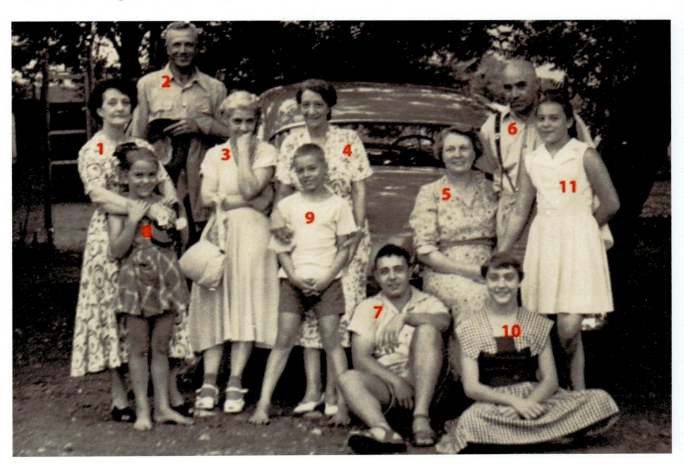

1Mali, 2 Tiny Faure,3 Issie Wiid,4 Heilie,5 Lucie,6 Johann, 7 Louw Wiid, 8 Tilla, 9 Philippus, 10 Martha, 11 Hilet Badenhorst (7 = son van 3) (8,9,10&11 Johan's children) Kaap Muiden farm belonged to Badenhorst&Wiid (Company) It never belonged to Philippus C. Badenhorst. Johan and deWetWiid farmed together on KaapMuiden.) Lourens de Jager Wiid, brother of deWet Wiid sold his portion of the farm. De Wet Widd bought his own farm at Coopersdal, Komatipoort.

Daughter of Johan Badenhorst *1943 Studied Education Diploma.

She was married 3 times and had 2 or 3 children.

BOND STREET DAYS

This photo was taken in 1948 and I always thought the man on the far right was a
Badenhorst, who were much younger than my father and I incorrectly assumed it was
my father's uncle. (Everyone older than yourself in those days were called "uncle".

I met his daughter on Geni and later on Facebook and when she saw the photo, she confirmed it was her father, the son of Issie (1/2 sister to my grandmother, married to a Wiid).

Bond Street 10, I remember well as we stayed there in a room for one or two years. It was at the lower end of Lynnwood road, between the "Hervormde" church and "Afrikaans Hoër Seunskool". You turned left and immediately right into the street. Bond Street was only 200 to 300 metres long.

The Boarding house had double doors. Once inside there was a large hall, with steps to the left and right ending up together on a landing. On the far end on the ground floor, there were passages to the left and right. Straight ahead led into the guest dining room, with double doors. There were rooms leading off the hall on both sides. The passage on the ground floor towards the right led to the bathrooms and towards the left led to the kitchen, and my grandmother's room if you turned left again at the end of the passage. We were never allowed anywhere near to my grandmother's room. On the top of the stairs, on the landing, there were passages leading to all the different rooms. At this time all the rooms were allocated to each of her children with a few rooms reserved for guests. There were at least 10 rooms, some on top of the dining room, which had to be kept empty during dinner time. There were visiting diners from elsewhere. Outside at the front there was a big lawn. On the left there was a gravel road leading to the back with parking spaces for all the cars and a big blue gum tree at the end. A mulberry tree to the right, with a Lateria bush underneath, sometimes the flowers were used as confetti, but it could stain, so it wasn't popular. You could watch the girls of the Girl school during their school breaks and had to explain your stained clothes when it was fruit bearing. The blue gum tree was used as a zip wire with a smooth steel wire tied to the tree towards a pin in the ground. A piece of water pipe was inserted with a cloth over it to save your hands from getting trapped between the pipe and the wire. Later they tied the far end of the wire somewhere higher up to slow down the slide at the end. It was happy days until someone sprained an ankle and the wire was taken down.

In order to save water, we had to bath with one of my father's sister's boys until he crapped in the bath and we jumped out of the bath like it was struck by lightning – it was the last time.

On another occasion, this same cousin ran excitedly to my grandmother and cried "Granny, Granny!" "Yes my child" on which he continued "Gran, did Gran know Ounooi's arse is so deep" indicating on his finger just how deep it was. "Sis" she said "I'll have to wash out your mouth with soap and water – now go wash your hands immediately!" Ounooi was the families' "boerboel" bitch. (boerboel = Ridgeback)

We often pilfered dough while my grandmother was baking, to her dismay. We later gave it back after we had sculpted it into various forms like settees, etc. She baked it for us and the result were contorted pieces of bread, which we ate while they were still nice and warm.

Uncle Farrell had such a car, a 1945 Hudson Terraplane, but his was a beige colour with the same canvas top cover and Running boards with the spare wheel built into the front mud guards.

Uncle Klammie had a smaller car with a dickie seat which could take 2 passengers with the spare wheel at the back of the boot. He apparently courted my grandmother when my grandfather was out of town, but my grandmother couldn't stand him, unless there was no one there.

When my uncle turned into the grounds my older cousins would jump onto the running boards and hitched a ride.

MY DAD

My Dad was one of a big family of 10 children. He was the eighth child and was given to his oldest sister to be raised. She was quite upset about the "gift".

While at school he excelled at prose. There wasn't money for a formal university education and he continued his education in a technical school, where he achieved the highest marks for mathematics in the Transvaal. He enrolled for an apprenticeship as a photochemical engraver with the state printer of Pretoria and later for the Dagbreek Printing works.

He taught me to work with my hands in case I was not able to make the grade at university. He was so convinced that I would not make my first year at university, that he bet my mother R20.00 that I wouldn't make it. With my 2nd year he did not repeat his bet and I got stuck in the gate. (It was easier the 2nd time)

My father was a big DIY enthusiast. While he was living on our small holding, he built the chicken runs, lined the water tank, to make the water safer and more palatable and installed a water system with piping to the house. He built a septic tank complete with dead cat. He converted a budgie cage into a cooler by making a double layer in the walls, filled with charcoal and an inside layer of linen cloth with a dripping tray, from which water drip onto the charcoal for evaporative cooling. He also repeated this effort on my mother's parent's farm. The butter was cold enough to prevent it from being spread.

Later he installed a Wolseley engine with an "alternator" and panel board with meters and an engine stop inside the house, so that we had electrical power in the evenings as well as a fridge that remained cold if you didn't keep on opening the doors.

He then built his own arc welder with a choke and varied contact point for power adjustments.

With that he built a warm water system by fitting a boiler around the Aga stove's fire pot. He got the Aga from his parents when the boarding house was sold. The boiler was connected to a warm water storage tank that was heated by convection from the boiler to the loft and warm water pipes to the kitchen and bathroom taps.

He overhauled all his own car engines and once had a Norton motor cycle until he chickened out due to its excessive power.

His philosophy was that if he could learn his own trade, he can also acquire the knowhow to learn any other trade. He mostly learned from pamphlets and "Everyday Mechanic" to do what he sets out to do. He was handy and had good methodology.

His biggest downfall was his drinking habits, but he knew his limits. My mother unfortunately could not say the same.

To his defence I can only mention that his in-laws judged him on his absence of religious conviction and his lack of a university education.

MY JOUBERT FAMILY

The genealogy of the Jouberts and the Pretorius family is interwoven due to my grandfather Joubert's mother being a Pretorius, linked to the family of my grandmother so I discuss them in combination.

My own matrilinear line (Mother's mother's mother etc.) with MTDNA was initially incorrect when compared to other people that had a link to a J-2a1a1e haplo group until I made the breakthrough.

(I did a mt-DNA and tested as J-2a1a1e.)

The true matrilinear line is thus:

My **mother**, Rachel Jacoba Joubert, born 1/8/1922 will have the same haplogroup as me and so will my maternal **grandmother** Rachel Jacoba Pretorius, born 18/1/1882, who was one of a twin and had a twin herself. (Three twins in my whole family.)

My maternal **great grandmother** was Magrietha Petronella Maria de Wet, born 1857, married to Johannes Lodewikus Pretorius, born 1858.

2x great grandmother was Rachel Jacoba Pretorius, born 1838 x Jan Harm de Wet.

3x great grandmother was Anna Elizabeth Margaretha Robbertse x Johannes Lodewikus Pretorius.

4x great grandmother was Anna Elizabeth de Beer x Daniël Jacobus Robbertse.

5x great grandmother was Cornelia Nel X Johannes Mattheus de Beer.

6x great grandmother Cornelia van Jaarsveld b8 1728 x Ferdinandus Nel.

7x great grandmother Cornelia Nel born 1690 x Adriaan Arij van Jaarsveld.

8x great grandmother Jean de la Batte, born 1662 x Guillaume Willem Nel, Progenitor.

Her mother was Susanne Vyette Laurent. X Jacques de la Batte.

(You can either say great great great great and count it on your fingers or 2x 3x 4x great grandparents)

All these people are mt DNA J-2a1a1e and several descendant lines (more than 3 exist) with Jeanne de la Batt as MRCA and testing as Mt DNA J-2a1a1e. Thus, my matrilinear line has been proven.

Hendrik Stephanus Pretorius b5c3d5e10, born 1792, was the **MRCA** between my mother's father and my mother's mother. **My great - great - great - great - grandfather** on my grandmother's side (mother's mother) He was also **My great - great - great -grandfather,** on my mother's **father's** side (He was thus his own father!)

His granddaughter was Elsie Magdalena Carolina Pretorius b5c3d5e10**f5g9,** my grandfather's mother and my great grandmother.

Hendrik Stephanus Pretorius b5c3d5e10 *1792

Johannes Lodewikus Pretorius b5c3d5e10f1 Daniël Pieter Pretorius b5c3d5e10f5

Hendrik Stephanus Pretorius b5c3d5e10f1g2 Rachel Jacoba Pretorius b5c3d5e10f1g3 and their cousin, Elsie M. C. Pretorius b5c3d5e10f5g9, Daughter of D P Pretorius above.

Johannes Lodewikus Pretorius b5c3d5e10f1g2h2 **X** Magrietha Petronella Maria de Wet, daughter of R.J. Pretorius b5c3d5e10f1g3.

Daniël Pieter Joubert **grandfather** son of EMC Pretorius e10f5g9 marry

Rachel Jacoba Pretorius b5c3d5e10f1g2h2i1 **grandmother**

My grandmother's parents on my mother's side were first cousins and my maternal grandfather, Joubert, married his 2nd cousin's daughter. (Mother's cousin's grandchild.)

The grandson of Hendrik Stephanus Pretorius b5c3d6e10* 1792 was **Hendrik Stephanus b5c3d5e10f1g2,** *1836, a cousin of Elsie Magdalena Carolina Pretorius b5c3d5e10**f5g9**.

The Member of parliament, Hendrik Stephanus Pretorius b5c3d5e10f1g2. *1836

This member of parliament was also my grandmothers, Rachel Pretorius b5c3d5e10**f1g2h2i1's** grandfather, or the father of Johannes Lodewikus Pretorius b5c3d5e10**f1g2h2**, (the father of my grandmother.)

Hendrik Stephanus Pretorius b5c3d5e10's (*1792) other grandchild, **Rachel Jacoba Pretorius** b5c3d5e10**f1g3**, or the sister of this member of parliament, was my grandfather's aunt and also the grandmother of my grandmother, Rachel Jacoba (Her mother's mother), thus Magrietha Maria Petronella de Wet's mother. This Rachel Jacoba was married to Jan Harm de Wet. (Thus, Magrietha and Johannes Lodewikus were first cousins)

Elsie Magdalena Carolina Pretorius b5c3d5e10f5g9, born 29 Sep 1856 in
Roodewal, Standerton and died 24 Nov 1936 in Hazeldene, Pretoria.

Her mother's sister, Aletta Magdalena Smit, was married to Marthinus Wessel Pretorius, the founder of Pretoria.

Grandfather Daniël Pieter Joubert, born 1877.On the 2nd photo with his younger
brother, Johannes Willem Jacobus. In a photo taken in 1907, they were 20 and
19 years old, at their mother's 2nd wedding to Willem Carel Meyer.

Hendrik Stephanus Pretorius b5c3d5e10, *1792 married to Rachel Jacoba Liebenberg, is the Most Recent Common Ancestor (MRCA) between my grandfather Joubert and my grandmother Pretorius.

(He was the Great great grandfather of my grandmother Pretorius and the great grandfather of my grandfather Joubert.)

My grandfather Joubert's grandfather, Daniël Pieter Pretorius (Elsie Magdalena Carolina Pretorius's father) and my grandmother Pretorius's great grandfather, Johannes Lodewikus Pretorius, were brothers. (See the diagram under the Pretorius Family.)

Grandfather Joubert had such an old 1938 Ford Humpback with 2 small rear windows and Running boards with 4 doors. My Dad overhauled its engine, had the cylinder sleeves line bored and installed new oversize pistons and rings. My Dad ground the valves and seated them. When finished he had spare parts left but got the car going anyway. Grandfather Joubert was adamant that no smaller car would pass him and once he almost went off a drif when a wagon with oxen was already on the bridge. (Drif = slightly raised bridge.)

Jopie Johannes Fourie who got shot by the English by a firing squad after the end of the Anglo-Boer war of 1898. His father was Joseph

Johannes Fourie b19c5d2e2f? * 1850. His Mother was Anna Margaretha Sophia Pretorius, the youngest sister of Elsie Magdalena Carolina Pretorius, my grandfather's mother. He was thus my grandfather's first cousin. He was married to Susanna Pistorius, 1880 – 1952. They had a daughter who was later married to a Strydom and they had a son, Dirkie Strydom.

Elsie Magdalena Carolina Pretorius's mother was Jacoba Stephina Smit *1822, married to Daniël Pieter Pretorius and her mother's **sister, Aletta Magdalena Smit *1818** was married to **Marthinus Wessel Pretorius*1819**, the founder of Pretoria.

Aletta Magdalena Smit (sister of grandfather Joubert's mother's mother, Jacoba Stephina Smit), married to Martinus Wessel Pretorius, the founder of Pretoria. (No photo available of Jacoba Stephina Smit)

Marthinus Wessel Pretorius *1819, Founder of Pretoria. (**b3c1d5e12f1**). Pretoria was named after his Father, Andries Wilhelmus Jacobus Pretorius born 1798, who retaliated at the battle of the Bloodriver on 16 December 1838, following the murder of Piet Retief and his comrades, that took place on 6 February 1838 at Umgungundlovu after Retief signed an agreement.

Marthinus Wessel was thus my great grandmother, Elsie Magdalena Carolina Pretorius's uncle. His children were my great grandmother's cousins. = Married on family.

He was married on family as well as **bloodline** family, with **Johannes Pretorius the progenitor as MRCA** between him and the mother of my grandfather, **Elsie Magdalena Carolina Pretorius b5c3d5e10f5g9 = 6 generations back and then forwards again.**

Although aunt Ita, my mother's sister marked this photo as Stephina, I recognised her as Aunt Sophie (**Sophia Jacomina van der Walt *1890**) who lived in the direction of Swaelpoort from Mooiplaas. You had to pass over a flooded drif. My brother or I had to walk in front of the car to prevent my father from going over the edge of the drif. Her husband was **Hendrik Stephanus Pretorius Joubert**, one of my grand father's younger brothers ***1887**.

They were the parents of Burt Joubert who was married to his cousin Stella Wolmarans. I was in touch with Hendrik's grandson, (His son Johannes's son) and he confirmed the photo as his grandparents. He has taken over their farm. He was not very communicative and I could not find out much more about Uncle Burt Joubert (My mother's cousin), except that Stella's surname was Wolmarans. (There were 2 old ladies who also stayed there. Also family.)

Burgert Frederik Joubert, (son of grandfather Joubert's brother) and Stella
Wolmerans, his cousin, at their wedding after 1945. They had no children.

I have known them both. He had sawmills in Rustenburg and Thabazimbië. He was my mother's first cousin. He talked with a falsetto voice and what impressed me at the time was his big varicosities on his legs. They both loved children.

My grandfather Joubert always told me that he was family of Martinus Wessel Pretorius, but I only found out after doing my genealogy in which way they were family. Marthinus Wessel Pretorius was married to his mother's mother's sister. (Blood family, back to the Pretorius progenitor.)

Grandfather Joubert had a horse saddle which hung over a beam in his garage and he also kept his set of spurs that he used during the Anglo-Boer war. His wish was that his children would donate them to the war museum.

He always smoked his pipe filled with "Assegaai" tobacco. My dad always provided him with Rum and Maple tobacco to mix, which was less strong. One of his home remedies for toothache was to smear some of his pipe oil onto the offending tooth to ease the pain. He also used snuff tobacco as well as chewing tobacco. He had a pocket knife that was ground into a hollow curve, that he used for anything from cleaning his pipe to cutting a sheep's throat, cutting beef hides or to cut biltong. (One of his pipes was cleaned until there was a hole through the bowl).

He got up at the break of dawn, went to the stables to look after the milking and to see to all the farm animals feeding. Afterwards he sat on the veranda with a cup of coffee until everyone else started moving, and making ready for breakfast. He never asked for help but accepted it if it was offered. He never talked about the war and said he had sworn an oath. He always said that a son was not a man before he had shot a lion on his own. One of his favourite past-times was to define family ties and he could go back to 3 or 4 generations.

Grandfather Joubert always listened to the church service on Sundays on his radio that operated on car batteries. The batteries had to be charged beforehand with a Brigs and Stratton engine and generator. Eventually it would not charge anymore and my dad came to the rescue by taking everything apart, cleaning the commutator, installing new brushes, taking the batteries apart, getting rid of the sediment and refilling it with acid, resealing it and then recharged the battery. Throwing it away and buying a new one was not an option as it was not long after the 2nd World War, when everything was scarce or very expensive. Thus after a whole day he got everything going. To test it all he switched on the radio and Louis Armstrong sang one of his better numbers. My grandfather remarked how beautiful the man sang, but when my father pointed out to him it was an American black, he was so disgruntled, he switched the radio off immediately and didn't talk to anyone for 3 hours.

Sunday meals on the farm were an occasion not to be missed. The dining room was always kept in the dark to lessen the flies. The curtains were then opened and the dining room table was enlarged by cranking it open for a spare table surface to be added and cranked close to make it sturdy again.

The table was covered with a clean starched table cloth and the table laid with dinner plates, side plates and cutlery including fish knives, bread knives, meat knives and all the forks and spoons – the serving spoons were silver. Serviettes had serviette rings, or were folded to make them stand upright.

The serving dishes were then brought in. The meat dish was offered to the head of the family who could ask a subservient person to carve the meat.

With one of the Sunday meals after the table prayer in Dutch "Segen Vader die voedsel wat U voortgesit het, Laat ons U nimmer vergeten." The kitchen servant asked if he could bring in the dead chicken. My mother's brother was adamant he wasn't going to eat it, as he didn't eat dead chicken.

With weight loss in mind, there once were green salads on the menu but my grandfather refused to eat it "I'm not a goat!" he said.

The plates and cutlery was kept in a side board in the dining room.

Most of the farm visits occurred over a weekend and after Sunday dinner all the old people had a siesta and the children also had to sleep, if they wanted to or not. That was when we escaped through the sash windows, when we were sure everyone else was asleep, to breathe the fresh air, to listen to the silence and the doves cooing until we got bored. We started to think of other things to do, so that was when we pilfered conserve destined for sweets after dinner. You had to eat a whole bottle, wash it and put the empty amongst all the other empties, so that no one would realise there was anything amiss. Then you had to get back through the window and wait for everyone else to start moving.

Your best possession was your pocket knife. With that you could cut off a branch from a tree if you sprained an ankle, when you are away from home. It was also a weapon if you got attacked, which in those days was only a theoretic consideration. I remember I once killed a snake and skinned it. Then dried the skin with salt, spreading it out. I kept it for quite a while.

The hilly outcrop, covered in boulders, some distance from the farmyard was another pastime when we visited the farm. We jumped from boulder to boulder downhill until we could do it at speed, oblivious to any danger of injury. The big rock, at the end of the outcrop was considered as a no-go area but we climbed it regularly to watch the world from on-top of it.

When you walked to the beacon a bit further on, you could see the borders of the farm lining it up to the next beacon far away. This imaginary line was sometimes fenced in, but not always. The farm was further divided into enclosures for the sheep and cattle. In the pioneering days the size of a farm was determined by the area you could travel around on horseback from sunrise to sunset.

One American farmer said that they do it by motorcar, whereupon the South African remarked "Shame, I also once had a car like that. Later with subdivision the farms got smaller and smaller and less economical and ended up in subsistence farming for own use only. At some stage previously my grandparents tried their luck on the diamond fields but were unsuccessful.

It was during these visits that I gained first-hand what "dolosse" were. It was the calcaneus of cattle and represented oxen and the phalanges representing the herders. The lower jaw of a sheep (mandible) was used as the wagon and the oxen was then spanned in in front of the wagon with tied up string. Eventually you had a whole team of oxen. Later I learned to make clay oxen that needed much less imagination. A stick served as yoke with string as strops.

You rolled a piece of clay in a cone, the width of your hand – in the middle was the front legs which you pinched up and divided into two The back became the hind legs by bending it down and dividing it into two – The front end you divide into 3 for the horns and face. By pressing the front end of the back you created a hump. Now you could sculpt it into the ox by rubbing and stroking the clay into all the desired features, like tail or male organs if you dared.

Clay oxen and cart made with modern clay.

With holidays we went on walks with Aunt Ita (My mother's sister) with the farm dogs. Firstly you had to inhale deeply and blow it all out for 5 minutes before you could begin walking. I never walked with my grandfather.

On one occasion I went with my father and grandfather to the pig sty. The pig jumped up onto the gate and I got a fright and shouted out "Good God, you bloody pig!" My grandfather then wanted to know from my father where I learned to talk like that.

My grandfather towards the end of his life, developed cancer of his lip from smoking a pipe, which was treated successfully with surgery. He was also coughing a lot but he had written it off as due to all the days in the veld during the Anglo-Boer war. Apart from that he never talked of the war and said he had sworn an oath not to talk about the war. His own cousin was executed by a firing squad. (Jopie Fourie – his mother's youngest sister's son.)

In the end he developed heart failure and was given bedrest with medication, before he ended up in hospital where he died. He was the first corpse I had ever seen and I remember my mother kissing him on his forehead. His coffin was open for everyone queuing up to say their goodbyes.

He was placed in a hearse and everyone followed on foot half a mile to the farm cemetery where he was given his last resting place. One of the Joubert sons had to get into the grave with him to sort out a hitch with the coffin release mechanism. The farm folk stood in a row with their hats in their hands in the background.

Afterwards the will was read to a selected audience followed by a stampede to claim personal effects like a lot of vultures.

This was followed by a big feast and coffee drinking, with everyone talking over each other at the same time. I saw some of my cousins that I hadn't seen in quite a while. I could not understand the jollity. This was when I was in standard 5 and I was 12 years old.

My brother, Joubert, met one of grandfather Joubert's family a "Rooi Jan" when my father acquired a Plymouth motor car.

I remember the one with the hat and later when I learned of "Ampie en Sampie" in Afrikaans prose I managed to recall him.

To be given up with Railway Ticket on termination of journey.

Form M.T. 5. No. 62794

AUTHORITY TO TRAVEL.

THIS IS NOT A RAILWAY TICKET.

Place... *Umbilo Camp*

Date... *28 Aug 1902*

The Bearer* *D. P. Joubert*

with | ...... has authority to

proceed by rail from *Durban* to *Pretoria*

on *28th Aug 2* and return on...

Rationed at...

To and for...

Name...

Rank...

(Signature of Issuing Officer).

*Here enter Rank, Name and Regiment if an Officer or Soldier, and Name and Department if a Camp Follower.

|Here enter number of persons travelling.

NOTE.- This Form must be retained by the person travelling, and be produced by him whenever called upon to do so.

Rudolf Steger DP Joubert PRE South

A few months after the end of the Anglo-Boer war, with my grandfather's discharge
from the Umbilo concentration camp, he got a permit to travel from Durban to Pretoria.
His future wife was not far from there in the Merebank concentration camp.

He was in Umbilo for 6 months from 3/2/1902 until 28/8/1902 after being captured in Brakpan. His number was 28064. The peace accord was on 31st May 1902 and he was only released 3 months afterwards.

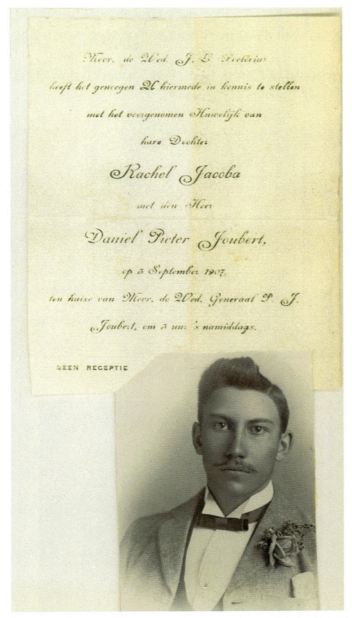

Wedding invitation of Grandfather Joubert and grandmother
Pretorius at the house of Komd. Genl. P.J Joubert.

Comd. Genl. Piet Joubert had died at this stage, so it was actually the house of his widow. (But there was a farm house, as well as a town house. Not sure which one it was.)

The town house and Farmstead of Comd. Genl. Piet Joubert below. The town house later became "Meisies Hoër" .

Town house.

Farm house of Comd. Genl. P. J. Joubert, who was part of the family.

KRYGSGEVANGENES

BYGEWERK 2013/07/03		FOUT / NOTA / REBEL / 2de BLS / EED

FOTO — JA

NOMMER	VAN	NAAM	OUDERDOM	GEBOORTEDATUM
28064	JOUBERT	DANIÉL PIETER	24	

ADRES	DISTRIK	NASIONALITEIT	RANG
MOOIPLAATS	PRETORIA	Z A	

FOTO NO	PLASING OP FOTO	WAAR IS FOTO GENEEM
PETER BOSHOFF		

WAAR GEVANG?	WANNEER?	KOMMANDO	VELDKORNETSKAP
BRAKPAN	1902/02/03		PRETORIA

SUID-AFRIKA :

SUID-AFRIKA	DATUM VERSKUIF	KONSENTRASIEKAMP	KK KAMP IN SA
DURBAN		Onbekend	UMBILO

DATUM VERSKUIF [2]	KONSENTRASIEKAMP 2	DATUM VERSKUIF [3]	KONSENTRASIEKAMP [3

OORSEE :

SKIP	DATUM SKIP VERTREK	DATUM AANKOMS	LAND

KGV - KAMP	2DE DATUM VERSKUIF	KAMP NO 2 / NOTA	TENT / HUT NO

STERFPLEK :

	DATUM OORLEDE	OORSAAK VAN DOOD
KGV / KK KAMP / JA		
AAN BOORD-SKIP	ELDERS - WAAR?	WAAR BEGRAWE?
ELDERS		

TERUGKEER :

PAROOL	DATUM EED AFGELÉ	SKIP TERUG NA S.A.	DATUM-TERUG NA S.A.	DATUM IN SA

DATA
DURBAN

GROEPFOTO / SKIP / OF ANDER — LAND / KAMP

A certificate from the SA war museum after I sent them a copy of his photo and particulars with his prison number. (krygsnommer.)

They confirmed that after the date he was captured, no prisoners were sent to Ceylon. He was thus never in Ceylon and the family folklore was wrong.

A Bone ring, made in Ceylon, was made by the former fiancé of grandmother Pretorius. (She was engaged to someone else before she married Grandfather Joubert.)

MY PRETORIUS FAMILY

Johannes Lodewikus Pretorius, The father of my grandmother Pretorius. Born in 1858. Died 1907.

Johannes Lodewikus Pretories was remarried in 1904 to Cornelia Susanna Joubert, but had no children with her. She had a child from her first marriage Cornelia Susanna Jacoba Jordaan, the same age as my grandmother.

He forced my grandmother's twin, Gerbrecht Susanna to marry at age 13 years old. She was pregnant and died after childbirth. She was buried 1895 in a grave with the text on the reverse of the headstone. He has sworn everyone to secrecy and forbade anyone to talk about her.

My grandmother knew all about it as she was there and she told me when I was about 10 years old. She confirmed that the baby was born alive and that the husband was too useless to raise the baby himself. I assumed the baby was given up for adoption. I couldn't find any records as it would be confidential and only the adopted child would have been able to access the records. He had 9 children all together.

My grandmother's twin, Gerbrecht Susanna at her shotgun marriage, who died during childbirth. According to my grandmother the child survived. No one knew what happened to the child. I could not find her marriage certificate, death notice or birth record and it may fore-ever remain a mystery.

My great grandmother Magrieta Petronella Maria de Wet, born 1857 married Johannes Lodewikus Pretorius on 8/12/1879. died 23 April 1902 in Merebank Concentration from Appendicitis. She and her husband were first cousins. Also known as Mita.

Matthys Gerhardus Pretorius born 1861, a brother of Johannes Lodewikus
Pretorius *1857. My grandmother Pretorius' uncle.

Elsie Magdalena Carolina Pretorius *1856, grandfather Joubert's mother and
the cousin of Magritha's mother, Rachel Jacoba Pretorius*1836.

Also the cousin of Johannes Lodewikus Pretorius's (*1858) father, Hendrik Stephanus Pretorius *1835. A big age difference between her and her cousin, because she was the 9th child of Daniël Pieter Pretorius *1821, who was the 5th child of Hendrik Stephanus Pretorius *1792, while her male and female cousin stem from the oldest son, Johannes Lodewikus *1814. My grandmother Joubert liked her very much.

Cornelia Jordaan was the same age as my grandmother and came into the household when her mother, (the widow of Gerhardus Joubert), remarried Johannes Lodewikus Pretorius in 1904, when he became a widower. She knew all the Jouberts as she lived with her mother during her mother's first marriage.

She was a "step" cousin to my grandfather Joubert and most likely introduced him and my grandmother to each other after my grandmother Pretorius broke off her engagement, with the chap that was in Ceylon, who gave her a handcrafted bone ring.

Magrietha on the left and her husband on far right. Don't know who the bride and groom were.

Rachel Pretorius at her wedding to Daniël Pieter Joubert in 1907.

Left top my grandmother on the left at 13 years of age with her twin sister, who overstepped the mark and paid with her life for it by dying in childbirth. On the right my maternal grandmother at age 18 just before being sent to the concentration camp.

On this photo my grandmother as nurse in the Merebank concentration camp at age 20 years in 1902. Her sister Elsie Magdalena Adriana died there at age 10 on 3 Dec 1901 and her mother died on 23rd April 1902 at the age 45 years from peritonitis.

My grandmother sitting on left front at age 20, with her younger brother, Hendrik
Stephanus Pretorius born in 1883, 19 year old on photo, followed by Jan Harm
Pretorius, born 1886, 16 years old. In front right, Johanna Lodewika Pretorius, born
1893, 9 yr old on photo. Photo taken just after the end of the war in 1902.

Magrietha Petronella Maria, born 1888, then 14, and Johannes Lodewikus born 1895, then 7 years old. Christoffel Johannes, born 1897, then 5 years old, not on the photo. Possibly separated as with the English policy at the time.

Elsie Magdalena Adriana, born 1891 died on 3/12/1901 in Merebank.

Magrietha Petronella Maria died on 23 April 1902 from Peritonitis, 5 weeks before the peace accord.

MY OWN STORY

Me in 2013, happily married to my second wife in England, to the dismay of some of my family who had not forgiven me for leaving my ex.

In the sheep enclosure on four inches of "clean" kraal manure to build up immunity, to protect me against infections before the advent of available antibiotics.

King of the castle in 1944, before my brother was born. For sixteen months I was the only child.

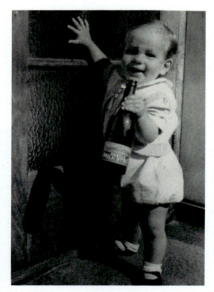

My first introduction to alcohol with an empty bottle of beer.

My father always told everyone that beer was good for children because it contained something that made them sleep.

Me comforting my brother with a pacifier.

In 1945 up to 1946, my parents, Joubert and I were in the Cape. It was in the immediate aftermath of the Second World War. I was nursed in a chest of drawers, and if I was good, they kept it open. My mother had to queue up to buy rations, and because she had a Jewish appearance, the shopkeepers often allowed her to jump the queue. By repeat storytelling, I know my mother once burned my nappies in an effort to dry them on the oven railing during the wet Cape weather. To mask the burn marks, she sprinkled it thickly with baby powder. This is possibly why I still now sneeze when I come anywhere close to talcum powder.

Me, before my first haircut.

My dad asked me to switch on the lights. It was a treat for him to watch how I was going to solve my task. I dragged a chair to the wall, climbed onto it to reach the switch, and switched it on without anyone ever giving me instructions on how to do it. (Before my hair was shaven off.)

My favourite playthings—a porridge spoon and a syrup tin which served as a bucket and a drum.

I could make a hell of a racket when I hit the tin with the spoon.

After my first hair cut at about 2.5 years old.

Joubert and me at a bench in Cape Town.

Joubert and me in 1946 on the flat balcony of Moulie point with Leeukop in the background.

At Anton van Wouw's sculpture which was dedicated to Commandant-General Piet Joubert's grandmother, Helena Susanna Strydom. (Her granddaughter, who resembled her, was a model. He also made use of a Jewish girl as model.) Helena was also my great-grandfather's grandmother, thus my great-great-great grandmother. Also an ancestor of Commandant-General Piet Joubert, mentioned earlier.

Joubert and me on Durban beach during a work assignment of my dad in 1949.

The motor gates with Joubert in 1951. When we learned to cycle, it was
our safety barrier in order to stop, and we simply drove into the gates.
Don't think there were brakes or maybe they didn't work.

Me in 1955 when I was in std. 4.

Clay shoot

For this you could use willow shoots or for a more robust clay shooter you could use a quince outshoot. My younger brother and I took turns picking from the farm youths to make up our teams. Their work was to gather clay below the ground dam wall and to knead it. The dam wall itself offered shelter, and the fountain, where the clay was, was open and exposed. We fired shots at one another for hours, but as we played we became more accurate, and this is when everything came to a head—with all the excitement and the farm youths joining in the fun and the clay blobs becoming bigger and bigger. After laughter comes tears. When Joubert got a big blob of clay right in the mouth we made peace with a sworn agreement that the adults wouldn't hear about our adventure. We realised that we could get hit in one of our eyes, so we agreed to stop any further clay adventures. One of my uncles were shot with a stone from a slingshot and he lost his one eye.

Ox Harnessing.

This was something noteworthy to remember. Excitement, panic, and fear in one emotion. I was trying to stay out of the way, but not wanting to miss anything. The event was announced ahead of time, two to three days after a good rain so that the soil was moist, but not too wet. The previous day the oxen weren't allowed out of the kraal, so they could calm down. The next morning, they were led out of the kraal with cow hide ropes around their horns to where the plough was, but it wasn't always easy. Rebellion was common, especially with the first endeavour of the season. There were shouts of encouragement, even louder shouts from my grandfather, who needed to control and coordinate everything - and with the whip cracking to encourage those who got stuck with all four legs anchored into the ground. The oxen bellowed until their vocal chords were raw, bucking with wide open red eyes in revolt, milling around and creating complete pandemonium with horns clattering on the yokes. Eventually the ones that were deemed to be uncontrollable were let loose and some order returned. Pairs of oxen got spanned with a greenhorn matched with an experienced ox under a yoke, with yoke spars each side of its neck and a strap underneath its neck. They then would be led to the plough in pairs and connected in order of experience and strength. The tamest went right in front, with a choice of the left- or right-hand side—the left-hand side was on solid ground, and the right-hand side was on ploughed soil, except for the first two rows. A youth was normally used as the tow leader. Then you had the whip handler with helpers alongside and the plough handler at the rear. The most important thing was to plough in straight lines; therefore, the tow leader needed to guide the oxen in a straight line. The plough handler needed to plough at an even depth. The whip handler sang out the ox names in rhyme: "Swartland, Redland, Transvaal, Freestate, Boland, and Grootland". And so forth. At resting periods, the oxen got fed and watered only enough to keep them going. As ploughing time was mostly warm, you had to look after your own water and wear a floppy-edged hat to keep the sun away from your neck. When I could demonstrate that I could walk in a straight line and keep up ahead of the oxen, I was given the opportunity to lead the team.

I must have been one of the last people to act as tow leader, and at the end of the season, I could also put my hand to the plough. It was not as easy as I thought it would be. Depending on the soil and the plough, there were between five and eight pairs of oxen.

This performance must be repeated two more times to rake the ploughed field and then with a planter to sow your crops.

(Oxen were replaced by horses and steam engines and later still by the modern tractors and even robotic tractors with GPS.)

For a lightly laden wagon on even roads, you needed four pairs of oxen; with a two-wheel scotch car, you only needed one pair. After this time, tractors took over, then there was no need for oxen, and they were consigned to history.

Ox Slaughter

Not as simple as you may think. It's much more than cutting a large chunk of meat into smaller parts.

Unless you try it yourself, you won't ever realise.

For starters, it depends on your livestock if you can afford to slaughter. I'm not talking of mega farms that slaughter on a commercial scale and take their cattle to an abattoir. I am talking of common, own-use farms, which after successive divisions over several generations since the 1940s were generally mixed farms with oxen for ploughing, a milk herd, a couple of pigs, a sheep flock, a coop of chickens, a fruit orchard, and a vegetable garden.

An ox can weigh from 750 to 1,000 kilograms. Afrikaner oxen are closer to the higher figure. The ox first had to be shot, away from the rest of the herd so as not to cause panic when the rest of them smelled the blood.

You could hardly shoot it from your front or rear veranda, and you couldn't load it over your shoulders and carry it home. You also couldn't shoot it in the kraal. You would choose your location and start negotiations with the farmhands on the neighbouring farm—to find out who was available with their labour in exchange for a share of the meat. You could then determine who did the shooting and how you would make the carcass lighter and more manageable.

On the day of the slaughter, everyone got up early and the ox was fed so that it didn't enter the afterlife with an empty stomach. The previous old people of bygone years were very adamant of that. You kept the ox in the selected area, usually under a big tree, and before wandering off he got shot. The ox was rolled onto a canvas and then hoisted up into the tree by his shanks and opened up and skinned. The entrails were then removed, and the edible portions like liver, heart, and kidneys were separated and taken home to the cooling room. This already reduced its weight by 30 per cent. The hind legs, shoulder blades, and front legs were then taken off, and then the head with horns attached could be removed. The carcass could then be sawn into halves over the length of the carcass, and the ribs were sawn off. The rest was then made into shorter portions which were taken home by wheel barrow. The rest was then taken home in a light scotch car or pulled home by manpower.

Meanwhile, the cooling room had been made ready by hanging wet sacks like a curtain and blocking all windows out to make it dark. The smaller portions were packed into a cool box. The box consisting of walls of double chicken mesh, two to three inches apart, and filled with charcoal onto which water drips from a dripping tray. The inside was lined with muslin cloth and wire racks to separate the contents. It stood on four legs to raise it from the ground.

The meat was hung up for 5 to 10 days to ripen and covered with nets to keep the flies off. Evaporative cooling, also helped by the darkness to isolate the heat from outside.

A pig could now be slaughtered, with much less drama and logistics for making sausages and dried out sausages. (Droë wors)

A pig has a very thick layer of dense fat and you needed to know how to shoot to kill it instantly with a Lee Metford gun. The meat was also hung up to ripen.

After the ripening process threshing tables covered with plastic tablecloths and fine netting were made ready. The workplace was a permanent frame work, with a roof made of reed, under a large tree. (Where the cooling box was also stationed.) The soil underneath was dampened, to limit dust and enhance coolness. This was swept regularly with a bush broom to keep it clean. The walls were enclosed on 3 sides with reed panels. Plenty of enamelled trays were put on the table, ready to prepare the meat.

Sections of the meat for short term use were selected and put in the cooler box. The ox tail was used to make oxtail soup.

All the knives were sharpened and honed and everyone was given a task.

The meat for the biltong was cut in strips and marinated in the trays over 24 hours. After marinating, it was hung up to dry. This became "biltong".

The meat for the sausages got cut up in smaller blocks ready to be ground, in a proportion of 3 parts of beef to 1 parts of pig, together with small blocks of fat and the whole lot seasoned with spices. It was ground 2 or 3 times before the actual sausage-making began, using processed sheep intestines. It was quite an art to feed the sausages evenly and co-ordination between the meat grinder and sausage maker was required.

Brawn was made from the offal by slow cooking and allowing to cool. It then was cut into slices for serving and could be made with or without curry powder.

The bones were cooked for soup and soap.

Caustic soda was added to make soap. The bony parts of the pig were also added and simmered in a large cast iron pot, standing more than 3 foot tall. The cleanly cooked bones were removed gradually. (The calcaneal bones were saved for the children to play with later) This method of cooking took a full day and then allowed to cool before cutting up into large rectangular blocks for drying out. "Farmer's soap". Too much caustic acid and the soap became biting and too little caustic soda, the soap became rancid.

The hooves and sinews got cooked to make glue.

A Massey Harris hand mill to grind chicken feed. By grinding white corn and grinding it twice and sieving it you could make corn meal.

When the mealies are still green, the husks and silk are removed to let them dry out and then the kernels are removed from the cob by a small hand corn thresher that you screw onto a table with a rotating wheel with serrations. (which you crank with a handle) The kernels are stored in a hessian sack. (You can also do it manually by taking one row off with your thumb and then rub two mealies on the cob together to get the kernels off from the cobs.)

The Massey Harris hand mill was operated by two people– one turned the handle while the other fed the mealie kernels into the funnel, and tied the sack onto the exit chute. This mill could provide enough flour for your own use and for feeding the chickens. (Then yellow mealies got used.)

In my mother's family all the children, except my mother became teachers. Her father also took part in the Anglo-Boer war and he was married to a Pretorius from Roodeplaat. This farm was on the far side of Pienaars river dam, close to Pretoria. My grandmother Joubert (Pretorius) was the grandchild of my grandfather's cousin. My grandfather's mother was also a Pretorius by birth. After my grandparent's wedding, post Anglo-Boer war, they settled on Mooiplaas, also near Pretoria, a self- sufficient farm for own use, 600 acres in extent.

I myself lived with my parents and brothers on a smallholding of 10 acres, close to Benoni. (1950's) with one cow, 2 pigs, 50 chicken with a rooster and a fruit orchard of 50 trees. From a young age my brother and I had to feed the chicken and collect all the eggs. We took turns between feeding the chickens, collecting eggs and milking the cow.

The cow's name was "Truitjie" the Afrikaans for Jersey as she was a Jersey cow. In order to milk her we had to cut arms full of pampas grass for her to eat, so that her udder and teats could relax. When she was restless she stood on your foot and you had to shoulder her to get her off. You had to be careful not to catch the hair in her udder, because she would kick out the bucket from between your knees. After you washed her whole udder and teats with soap water you smeared her teats with milkfat (a type of Vaseline). She gave about 2 gallon of milk a day, but it was very rich and creamy.

The milk was skimmed with a saucer from the bucket and collected separately. When there was enough cream you tipped it into a Kilner jar and shook it up and down by hand for about half an hour, to enable the butter and butter milk to separate. You poured off the butter milk and compressed the butter on a wooden board with a flat wooden spoon to get rid of any further butter milk and lightly salted it to taste. This was before anyone had heard of cholesterol and it was a part of your diet. You were active enough to burn off everything and "anything that didn't kill you made you fat".

In the autumn seasons we were selling fruit at the road side and although it was mostly free of grubs we had to prove it by giving a lusty bite into the fruit, hoping you didn't have half a worm in the other half.

With collecting eggs there were too many eggs to hold in your hands so you had to put some in your pockets. On one occasion there was a hooded cobra in the path between the chicken run and the kitchen. With a giant leap I jumped over the snake and ran into the kitchen, unfortunately I slipped on the step and most of the eggs smashed, with egg yolk running down my legs from my pockets onto the floor.

One of our pigs became ready for slaughter, but due to regulations you were not allowed to slaughter animals. Fortunately, it was close to Guy Fawkes night and my dad decided to wait for the first fire crackers to go off before he shot the pig with his pistol. Nobody was ever the wiser.

There wasn't any problem slaughtering a chicken. One farmhand delighted in chopping the chicken's head off and letting it run around headless before it died.

Our family frequently visited my grandmother's farm and during school breaks we would remain behind for our holidays. This was in the early 1950's when we were between 7 and 12 years old. We consolidated our farm and small holding experiences and became the last generation to experience the old traditional ways, before mechanisation and large scale farming took over. I wouldn't exchange my childhood days for anything and it is the reason why I still remember so much of it to this day.

RUSK AND BREAD BAKING

Almost anyone can bake rusks and bread in a modern stove with a thermostat and ventilation. You only need the recipe and an eye for detail.

It was a different kettle of fish to bake bread and rusks in an outside oven and you needed to hone your skills first. (Bearing in mind that the pioneers used termite heaps, hollowed out as ovens. The ovens of the day were raised and had a chimney with cast iron doors to allow easy access, keeping the heat within.)

The oven my grandmother used was an outside oven standing on an enclosed 3-foot platform under which the kindling and wooden logs were stored. The floor of the oven was concrete, lined with clay and the walls were clay bricks built into a dome, covered with a thick layer of clay inside and out. The chimney was at the rear and stood about 3 foot above the rest of the oven. The oven was, 3 feet wide and 4 feet long – it was closed off with a 12 by 18 inch cast iron door. My dad later made a valve to regulate the flow of the draught in the chimney.

The bread and rusk baking started the previous day when the flour was sieved and all the dry constituents were added – the dough mixed with a yeast plant (Kept going for years) Water or buttermilk was then added for the rusks. Then the kneading started and this was when you could gauge your strength against your grandmother – Things started off well until you ran out of stamina and that was when your grandmother needed to take over. The dough stood for an hour or two before the final kneading took place. It was covered warmly and left overnight to rise. The bread pans were put out and smeared with fat.

There was always a massive kettle on the stove, that was kept warm throughout the day for anyone that wanted coffee, or now and then tea.

Early the next day the fire was started outside the oven and while it got going the final kneading took place and the dough was placed in the bread pans and kept underneath blankets.

When there were enough glowing embers they were placed in the oven and spread over the whole length of the oven, with the oven door open a crack, and the chimney valve open. Extra embers were always on standby. When the oven was warm, measured by hand on the outside dome of the oven, the embers inside the oven were pushed to one side, the bread pans were loaded into the oven with a long handle, purpose made, flat spade.

The chimney valve then was closed, the time noted. If the oven was opened too early everything fell flat, waiting too long everything was dried out or even worse burnt. Over the years my grandmother got to know her oven and type of wood and mastered everything to a fine art. At last the time arrived and the first bread pan was taken out, with held in breath and tested. The rest of the bread pans followed and were carried to the kitchen and placed on wire racks to cool down. It was seldom that there was any problem with the end result, but with my father's interference the oven was more efficient so that some of the bread was surface burnt and he got the blame. The next time matters improved. My brother and I couldn't resist the fresh baked bread and rusks and had so much of it that we developed upset stomachs with resulting gas explosions, resulting in a horrible stench. (Farts.) When my mother's sister came into our room she visibly staggered and was appalled, before she rapidly disappeared. We will always remember her shocked face.

MY HIGHSHOOL YEARS OR
MY LYTTELTON YEARS

Me in std.8.

I saw my grandmother Badenhorst the last time in Park Street, Sunnyside in 1958, before she died from heart disease, this was two years after we moved to Lyttelton. (Later Verwoerdburg.) My paternal grandmother and grandfather already had been estranged at that stage and shortly after my grandmother's death he remarried.

There had always been a division between us brothers – my younger brother and me on one side, with the three youngest ones on the other. They had it easier than us, and took over most of our toys, but seen from the other side they got everything 2nd hand, while we were left with nothing.

We eventually got pocket money and in order to encourage us to save my father doubled any saved up money so that Joubert and I could buy worthwhile toys, while the younger ones spent all their money on sweets and couldn't understand where we got our money from.

My first interest in aeroplanes came from pictures, watching birds and insects, but especially swifts. I remembered my first dinky aeroplane for Christmas, which you could fly to and fro up and down, while you uttered an animated "eeaauw". Even in preschool you learnt to make paper planes to throw around and boats to play with. This reminds me of my primary school when the teacher told us the arithmetic test wouldn't count, so I folded my test paper afterwards into a plane and threw it around in class. When she gathered I didn't hand in my test paper she looked for it and unfolded my plane and saw I had 100% for the test.

My next stage in planes, were pre-cut balsa gliders, which could fly further than the paper models if they were balanced correctly and thrown in the correct way. I also remember building my own planes out of cigarette cartons with sticky tape – they looked right but couldn't fly.

The first model plane that could fly, was an aeroplane suspended on an arm with an electric motor with a propeller, by lever control it could even go up and down.

My next plane was a small Pee wee 0.025 cubic inch models flown from outside around a pole in the middle of the lawn – it was much faster and sounded like a hornet on steroids until it was replaced by U-control aeroplane models, starting with the Baby bee .049 cubic inch models right up to .35 cubic inch models, which bordered on dangerous and starting it by hand could do some serious injury. My largest U control was the 0.15 cubic inch motors model, which I learned to fly successfully. I even designed my own profile models (by setting the rudder on a permanent right deflection you kept the wires taught and the only other control you had was elevator up and down). You could fly loops, wing overs, where the model would go directly ahead from where you are standing. The next step was horizontal 8's – a loop, followed by an inverted loop. Before you flew you tested the controls showing up for elevator up and down for elevator down.

My father was holding the plane but not indicating any directions so I was gesticulating to him "Is the elevator up? Whereupon he released the plane, which made an instant loop, crashing immediately behind him. I also helped my brothers to fly as well. Their models were too heavy for the engines and just went in a low circle, hanging on the prop. So I designed a lighter model which responded to the controls, making a loop on full elevator, resulting in them crashing their planes and blaming me for a rubbish design.

The wings were constructed with a light balsa frame covered with tissue paper, painted in "dope" and duco with a layer of fuel proofer to prevent the duco from becoming all gooey. It had light plastic wheels.

The art was to fly with a stiff wrist and just moving your whole arm up and down for up and down elevator instead of just using your wrist, causing the plane to go rapidly up and down.

One of my cousins had flown a 0.35 model flew it on a large field when a drunk beggar wandered directly into the circle of flight. He could not decide whether to go up or down – down his plane would hit the ground and up he could hit him in the head, so he went straight and hit him on his buttocks. He fell over hitting the ground, motionless. Everyone was shouting, but before anyone could do anything, he jumped up and ran away.

My first "love disappointment" was with my primary school sweetheart who got herself pregnant with someone much older than her, at age 13 years, (She never knew how I felt about her or at least I never told her).

As it turned out I was a virgin until I got engaged at the age of 24. I had withdrawn from the opposite sex and everyone else with the excuse I needed to study. The result was that I became first for all the standard sixes in the whole school.

My dad sold the small holding and we moved to Lyttelton, later "Verwoerdburg" and at present Centurion. My dad had to travel daily to Jeppes Town so we had to be close to the railway line. He worked for "Dagbreek Pers Beperk Beserk" as my father called it and I travelled to my new high school, "Afrikaans Hoër" in the opposite direction towards Pretoria. From Pretoria station I got the steam train towards "Loftus Versveld", close to my high school. The only time you could see the mechanisms of propulsion, was when the train moved away. With the result that I was the last of the scholars to arrive at school. When the train was late, which happened quite often, everybody on the train was late and if you left your school bag on the train there was big trouble for you. The downside of travelling by train was that your collar and cuffs were always dirty from the soot, which was difficult to clean. Your clothes did not last long, which did not matter as you were growing out of them anyway. You were in a stage of rapid growth and had to get a replacement all the same.

One of the advantages of travelling by train was that you could do your homework on the train. After school with all the travelling and the walking to the stations and towards home, you were exhausted. What you couldn't do at home, you the cribbed on the train on your way to school the next day. My subject matter was aimed at university entrance with Latin, Mathematics, Biology, Science, Afrikaans and English.

The Latin teacher was called "Pappa". When you couldn't answer he always said "Come now Pappa, hold out your hands". You then got rapped over your knuckles with a ruler. The mathematics teacher was "Aap" as his initials were by chance A.P. The biology teacher was simply "Sir" as everybody liked him. The science teacher was "Pens" as he had a big stomach. The Afrikaans teacher was "draadtang" as he made do. The English teacher was called "Kraai" as his surname was Crause. The Principal was called "Phone" as he was as tall as a telephone pole.

The further you progressed, the more pranks were played. It was usually the other crowd, but you were implicated. Potassium permanganate crystals were the first to be tried out. On the train they were rubbed onto the door handle, between passenger wagons, while they were still wet and then allowed to dry out – when the conductor came along and wanted to go to the next wagon it exploded on touch like a fire cracker, not knowing what had hit him, he jumped aside, to the huge amusement of everyone involved.

A mixture of potassium, sulphur and a nitrate was a much more powerful concoction. It was wrapped in tin foil and when you dropped a stone onto it, it exploded like a gun shot. One of us went overboard by making a big ball, tightly wrapped in tinfoil and caused it to explode close to the school hall, resulting in one of the windows breaking from the shockwaves. It was a big carry on and the culprit barely escaped expulsion.

When you left the classroom to go to the toilet you walked past some of the classes (with everyone's voice having broken), you heard short bursts of laughter especially the Biology class. At one of the lessons the teacher explained that with evolution you lose certain parts of your anatomy or it got smaller, like your little toe, whereupon one of the wisecracks shouted out "We will exercise it in the meantime, sir". (Meaning a different organ.)

In the literature class the teacher wrote a comment on my essay "Good essay, but I don't like your theme", when I expressed myself a bit romantically in my essay.

To make things a bit more interesting our new Latin teacher sketched the Romans, as shooting each other with slingshots instead of using the correct term of catapults, which were much bigger. He also said that the Romans did not have electricity, so instead of executing the criminals in an electric chair they burnt them to death with candles.

Virgilius's love prose was popular when he described a deity as having breasts like two white doves.

One of my classmates just got the gist of the story in Latin and made up his own story instead of translating what was written.

With androgens rising, a number of the seniors teamed up by physically picking Pens's fiat 500 car and placed it in between 2 pillars with no hope whatsoever that he would be able to get out again without help.

I was never an athlete – with short distances it felt as if I was standing still and with long distances I got so short of breath that I had to abandon my attempts.

I imagined myself throwing a javelin a hundred metres or more, but when with my first attempt was only 10 metres, I was not even given the chance to try a second time. It was the one and only time in my life that I even held a javelin.

I then had to confine myself to cadet drilling and target shooting with a 0.22 gun.

My one cousin who's clothes I had to wear was always calling me names and humiliating me in front of classmates. I wrote him off there and then and promised him I would never ever speak to him again and I didn't.

Eventually I achieved a medical degree, while he never achieved anything despite all his father's money.

There were many firsts in my life – each new phase started with a first day. At the end of std. IX I got my first holiday job. At the end of each day I walked past a second hand shop and saw a moped scooter I liked, with a price I'll be able to afford at the end of my working holiday.

From then on I was trapped, as I had to look each day to see if it was still there. Time stood still, but eventually it was the end of the month with a works Christmas party thrown in as well. There was a woman that didn't like the men drinking so she poured all their brandies and whiskeys into the ice bucket. In order not to see it all wasted, I only drank ice water from then onwards.

I left early from the party. With mild intoxication and a swimming head I was off to the shop with my money in my pocket to buy the moped scooter. By now it was raining and the ice water started kicking in and I am, in the rain, with my first moped without a licence or registration off to Lyttelton. With my light headedness I didn't mind the rain. I didn't quite know how I got home, but I did, very proud of my moped.

I quickly gathered why I got it so cheap as the very next day I couldn't get it started. Sometimes it would miss or backfire but then nothing. I checked the point contacts, the sparkplug and cleaned the carburettor and eventually with the help of my dad, who suggested I check the key pin on the flywheel. I took off the flywheel and Bob's my uncle – I saw the key holding the flywheel in place was split and the flywheel not in the position it ought to be in. I sawed off a piece of steel to the right length and filed it to fit the key slot. With high hopes I tried starting it again and took it for a spin. Then my dad also wanted a spin. In front of the house the service road wasn't tarred and when my dad turned into our drive my moped went flying as well as my Dad. I stormed out and shouted "My bike, my bike!" My Dad asked me what about him. I was just relieved that the bike was still in one piece. I never found out what make the moped was or I couldn't remember as no-one has ever heard the name.

I'd taken out a provisional licence which was valid for a year and every time I had an appointment for my test, the bike gave notice. It had a help-me pedal and was unbelievably heavy. I converted it into a sportier version by just keeping the front mudguard and putting a bigger cog onto the engine side which made it weaker but once it built up speed was able to almost reach 30 mph downhill with an average of 20 mph.

With my matric farewell I could take a girl, but I didn't have a girlfriend. You had to ask the girl a month or more in advance and you had to be careful. The first one you asked had to say yes, otherwise she could find out she wasn't first choice and then you sat without a date. If you waited too long she didn't have enough time to get hold of a dress and you could be stranded on your own.

Eventually I picked a girl who was also in matric, and in all likelihood already had a dress. I still didn't have a driving licence and my dad had to take me to the school hall and bring me and the girlfriend back home. We were warned that the vultures (Traffic police.) would be on duty and were warned not to arrive without a licence. The accepted thing was to slip out towards the end during the closing speech and then continue the party elsewhere but unfortunately I hadn't organised anything. There we were all on our own having to wait for my Dad to pick us up. The girlfriend must have got fed up with me as she didn't want to see me after that, although I tried. During the speeches we all shouted "Yeah" or "boo" after each sentence and so my school time ended.

During my whole school career, I wasn't off sick for a single day and all the praise I got was the remark that I would make an excellent state service official.

Me during Matric 1961.

THE AIR FORCE GYMNASIUM

I applied for doing service in the air force gymnasium, so that I would not end up in the army camp as cannon fodder. I did however got exemption from the civil duty roster, but decided to have a break from studying.

Everyone was selected in the age group of 18 to 20 years, but with a huge difference in backgrounds. The basic training was for three months after which you got placed, dependant on which direction you wanted to pursue. I applied for training as a pilot, as I always wanted to fly myself, but due to my one eye being substandard I was rejected on medical grounds.

During the basic training you were chased around and did square bashing. We were told "Chest out, stomach in and in with your bum". They instructed us how to stand to attention. Coming to attention we were told that we sounded like a lot of cows that were peeing on a corrugated iron plate, except they didn't say peeing.

I had prepared for the gymnasium by regularly running for a mile which had helped me with my fitness level, but the days were long and in the evenings you were tired nonetheless. You still had to clean, wash and iron your kit. The overalls were washed in the laundry and you regularly got a clean one. You were constantly reminded that you were a nincompoop and lower than crayfish shit, which is lower than sea level.

Early each morning you got woken up with a bellowing and a banging on the metal door and you couldn't think you could turn over and sleep again. You had to wash the sleep from your eyes, brush your teeth, comb your hair. I got away without shaving for 2 months when the corporal looked at me attentively and asked if I was trying to grow a moustache. After ablutions you had to make your bed, exhibit your kit and wait for the daily inspection.

Your normal dress was your overall and you had to bone your boots with KIWI polish and spit so that they shone like a mirror.

The routine was regularly broken with manoeuvers, night marches and standing guard. We had regular PT (Physical Training) which consisted of running around and more running around, in between all the push ups and toe touching.

You were then asked if you were tired, if you confirmed it they said you were not yet fit enough and you had to run another circuit. If you came last, you have to run again. If you said you were not tired you needed to run again until you were tired. You couldn't win. After 30 push ups the corporal joined in and if you said you were tired, he asked you why he wasn't tired yet and you just had to continue.

We had a rugby player, of Springbok front row fame, who was a storeman in the gymnasium, also had a Springbok swimmer, a fellow who was a speed walker and another chap who was a boxer.

I had the honour to participate with the swimmer and it felt as if I had stopped swimming – he appeared to just skim on top of the water.

Then there was the walker – I figured if I could survive a chase parade that I could hold my own against him – the problem was that there were different rules and I was thrown out. When you fast-walked with him it felt as if you were walking and he was running, but with a heel-toe action. I developed a new respect for fast walkers.

The boxer was challenged by one of the corporals to a boxing match but it was held in private to prevent a dilemma in discipline.

Everybody found their niche in the end. I tried weight lifting but was messed around so much that I actually lost weight instead of gaining muscle. I was however selected for the President's guard as I had height in my favour. As guard you did duty one week each month, at the President's residence at the union buildings in Church street. I was the leader and with gun stamping on the ground you gave signals to your fellow guard what steps they had to follow. This was done with open bayonet.

Sundays, there was a church parade and I selected the Anglican church as you had tea afterwards where you could meet some of the local young ladies, which gave you the opportunity of chatting them up, but without success for me.

I also tried sharpshooting with our FN guns but I became so trigger happy with the semi-automatic that my overall score was actually quite low and only the very top was selected.

We also had the honour of lining Church street for Republic celebrations in 1961 and we were given the freedom of the city, but that was a scam and we very quickly were returned back to the camp.

At last it was the end of basic training and we had to choose which direction to follow.

As I failed the pilot medical, I chose radar operator, which would then allow you out of camp to the nearby airport, with a change of scenery. We were further selected after an examination for flight controllers in view of an air force career. As I had already decided to do medicine and I had university entrance, I did not try very hard to get selected and continued as radar operator at the PPI tubes.

Later in the year we were on an exercise at Devon airport to help the pilot trainees to complete a night training exercise. They had to do a 275 degree turn over a beacon, to the next turn over another beacon to get back to Dunnottar airport. One trainee did a 450 degree turn towards the hell and gone. It was not very long before he called our code name, admitting he was lost and needed help. The flight controllers made him turn in a circle to identify him from the other aeroplanes (Harvards) They had to direct him to another airport as he did not have enough fuel to get back to Devon. We then had to continue tracking him and the other aeroplanes on the radar screens while he was given bearings to follow to reach his alternative airport.

Our information was given over to a plotter, who plotted all their positions on a large chart, where each plane was given a number. A block representing each plane was then pushed around on the chart according to their positions. We were all delighted when the lost pilot landed his plane safely, especially the officers in charge of the exercise. One of the pilots landed without his landing gear extended and when they asked him why he didn't listen to the radio he said he could not hear it as the alarm was too loud.

Weekends everyone that did not have a pass watched movies – mostly war documentaries e.g. Battle of Britain or cowboy movies (Kick, shoot and table upending)- if you were not on guard duty.

I was proud of my military training and it gave me the strength of purpose, self-confidence and perseverance that I needed for the next phase in my life.

MY STUDENT YEARS

Like all students I also stated as a greenhorn. As I was not in a hostel and did not behave like a typical greenhorn by way of my confidence due to my military experience, I side stepped most of my "newbie initiations". Just keep yourself scarce, don't volunteer and don't push yourself into the foreground. During my first year I still had to make use of the train as my mode of transport.

The study work was very much like school, but much more work to do, and you had even more to learn by yourself from books, I also learned from the big shots. You had four subjects to pass – you chose one that was well formulated and systematic so that you could get promotion with a year mark of 75%, so you wouldn't need to do examination in that subject. Now you study hard for two other subjects and with three subjects to your credit you were eligible for a re-examination in the 4th, which you could now study on its own. This was Physics and as long as you attend all the practical laboratory sessions when roll call was held you would get a re-examination.

Having eventually passed all four subjects, you would most likely have to await selection for your second year, but enough students would fall away to give you a place to continue. During physics classes you could have a break and meet all the rugby players that got all the tips, being the favourites of the physics professor. I spent so much time in the cafeteria that I learnt to play bridge.

Wonder of wonders, everything worked out as planned – I got promoted in Botany, passed Animal studies and Chemistry and I got a re-examination in Physics

Somewhere in my first year I got my driver's licence, driving my father's VW-Combi, at the first attempt. We learned driving by sitting on my father's lap as small children, so that driving was second nature to us. Combined with all the times we "stole" my father's car for pleasure trips, we had adequate driving experience. One of the things my father drilled in us, was to stop on a ramp and to go slowly forwards and backwards by clutch and petrol pedal, once you released the handbrake. This all helped towards passing the licence testing.

With the half year holiday break I joined my family for the last time on holiday to Mosambique, here I netted my first German girlfriend, but I later learned she only used me to keep some undesirable blokes off her tail. I learned much later it requires much more than a platonic friendship to get a relationship going, but at that time I didn't know how to go about it.

After passing my first year tactically my Dad bought me a 1948 Morris 10 and we overhauled it together by having it line bored and giving it over sized pistons, grinding the valves for reseating them, buying new sparkplugs and points and "wallah", I had my own wheels. When it did not leak oil, it was because there was no oil left.

I started my 2nd year two weeks late. The tip for 2nd year was "Know all your work" I bought all my books, some second hand and I laughed when I looked at all the books piled up, thinking they couldn't be serious that I could learn everything. By the half year I realised it wasn't a joke and that I really needed to know everything explained in the books.

With my own wheels I was now independent and could now attend Rag week and helped building floats at one of the hostels. One float a day before the procession was only 25% completed and we had to work throughout the night to get it ready. One of my mates went to the Hatfield bakery at 0400 hours to get us sober and to encourage us to complete the float for the procession. We attended the procession red eyed to collect money from all the spectators.

After one of my classes I could not get my car started despite the fact that I knew it had enough petrol.

I called some of my classmates over to help push it. They pushed it back and forth several times when I noticed I hadn't switched the ignition on. Without telling them, I begged for one more push and within two yards the car fired into life and I waved them thank you through the window without stopping.

At the end of that year I went to work at Addington Hospital casualty department. With Waltzing Mathilda, as my car was baptised (There was 90 degrees of play on the steering wheel and it was difficult keeping it on the road – you depended on the kerb to keep it there.)

At Addington I learnt to insert stitches and after the year end party I got hopelessly drunk by partaking in drinking games under peer pressure. I was so drunk I could only speak English and when I woke up the next morning in the bath learned what it is to be Babbelaas (hungover). I was on duty but laid down where and when I could. It was one of the longest days of my life. It was the last time I was that drunk.

It was also during my 2nd year university that my father left home and from then I had to look after the household and my brothers in between my studies, so that I failed my 2nd year.

The repeat year was much easier than the first time round and I could ensure that I stayed on track. The foremost requirement was that you had to attend all your classes as all the professors knew you now and if you missed a class they officially welcomed you to the next class you attended.

It was during my repeat 2nd year that I met my first serious girlfriend. All my classmates stood on a corner where all the girls walked past and with each one walking past they rated her out of 10. They gave her a 7 but I gave her an eight.

I later met her in the cafeteria and started chatting to her and invited her to a play in our Aula theatre, which she accepted.

She invited me to her home in Waverley, Pretoria and we were on fire, but no sex. After a year we had a minor fallout and before anyone knew what had happened she got herself pregnant from a one-night stand. My second girlfriend I lost due to pregnancy by someone else. Her mother, who favoured me, invited me to her wedding. Many years later I heard that she had 2 children and her husband had a heart attack.

With the yearend, you could spot possible questions successfully in the written examination, but the fly in the ointment was the oral examination and no measure of waffling could help you out of the sewerage. The more you battled, the more they concentrate on your weak points. That was how I got stuck in the gate and had to redo that year. Like the one student saying he could answer the question better in English than Afrikaans, but still got stuck – so the professor said to him "Sir, I don't think you know the answer in Afrikaans or English"

Later during my 3rd year medicine, I saw my grandfather Boshoff for the last time. He was admitted to the orthopaedic ward after a road traffic accident with a broken femur. He stopped at a stop street and without looking he automatically continued on and caused the accident. He then was married to a Maria Jacomina Magrietha Matthyssen. I can remember meeting her once.

Now I started the clinical years of my medical training. It took a multitude of different people to fill the numbers. Some were wedded from the start, some started a second career. Some study themselves close to death, while others only study for the exams. I followed a middle way.

With other study courses you could change direction or choose different subjects and still obtain your degree, but with medicine it was more like a gamble and it was all or nothing once you started. Your only option was to complete your course or start something else altogether from scratch. Although once you are finished your course you could specialise to define your career in an alternative direction to general practice.

Luckily in those days we had good Bank managers. When you reached your clinical years, you could borrow against your future income and if you added enough to your study cost, you could even afford to buy a second hand car.

It happened that I gave my Morris to my brother for free and bought a VW beetle. It was a tomato red 1954 model. After I upgraded its engine, I had a good pair of wheels with which I could go on holiday or chase after the girls.

It was then that I met my future first wife and a year later we were married just before the beginning of my repeat 4th year medicine, no more chasing after girls and some stability. It was nice planning how to survive on her income and my loan money. From a student's perspective all you needed was an empty flat with a mattress to sleep on, a pair of bean bags to sit on, a second hand fridge and a stove hob with a few cooking pots. Bedside tables could be apple crates with a decorative cloth covering them. She decided to give up her flat and to stay at her parents to save money and to use the bus to get to work.

In this way by waiting and saving up we had enough money within a year, while we were engaged, to buy a proper bed and settee with a small fridge.

We had chosen a flat close to H.F Verwoerd hospital, where I have done the rest of my clinical years. It was close to the Pretoria Maternity hospital where I was born myself and delivered my first babies as a student. Also where my future brother in law was born on the same day as myself.

Taking lecture notes and lecturing is the passing of knowledge from one person to another without it going through the mind of either, and in my case a kind of shorthand that even I myself couldn't read it after a few years. A better way, was for you to prepare for a lecture and being able to ask questions after the lecture. Some lectures were presented in this way. One lecture I will never forget was one of our surgeons that went lyrical on how wonderful an organ the anus was – "It is the only valve in the world that can let gasses out and yet retain fluids and solids, but sometimes, just sometimes it doesn't quite work".

During examination one student was asked when someone is old. Without hesitation she answered "When someone is 10 years older than yourself" The professor was so chuffed with her answer that she was given a pass mark straight away.

The pharmacology professor always insisted that medicine is a poison, but by limiting the dose you can use the beneficial side effects, without doing damage, in other words any medicine in excess is dangerous.

My virology professor already in those times (1980) predicted that <u>viruses would become the pathogen of the future</u> and advocated a knowledge of viruses,

One of the professors said at a yearend party that a medical student when he had completed his studies was a learned barbarian, that didn't know much about life and hadn't built up any culture yet.

I had to give him evens. I learned a lot from my younger brothers working already and realised that I have some catching up to do, both in income and experience. They started off without a study debt and started earning at a much younger age – a double whammy. It would take me several years to catch up with them. The only thing in my favour would be that I worked much longer hours. The status you enjoyed as a newly qualified doctor made up for your lack of culture, until I came to UK and was made a nothing again, on par with freshly qualified doctors.

It was pressed on us students not to believe everything that you were told and neither what you read – you had to assess everything and decide on the benefit of everything, whether it was of use or not.

The biggest advantage of my medical training was to get schooled in clinical knowhow, to take and record a full medical history. I have gone through my whole medical career without getting a blot on my name. I'm not saying that I never made errors, but that I learned from my mistakes. Without support from your colleagues you are not worth much and that is where modern medicine falls short. Too many accusations and finger pointing.

After my final exam I told myself that I would never pick up any book to learn. How wrong I was. I even attained a further diploma at a different university. When you qualify the real learning starts.

MY INTERNSHIP AND FIRST YEARS IN PRACTICE

An internship is like starting your very first job. You now have to apply everything you have learned into practice in real life. You have to stick to rules, stay out of trouble and take on responsibility. I almost immediately started to make my own rule of thumb.

One of the first upsets was that in casualty my trousers got soaked in blood down the front, but as I had a tennis appointment I just quickly undressed and threw my clothes on the bed. My wife got the fright of her life when she got home as all she could see was blood and she did not know if I was ok.

After this followed a whole lot of firsts – First baby as doctor, first anaesthetic, first operation assisting, first operation done by myself.

I was already an expert in suturing, learnt in my student years and now I had a chance to improve my techniques. Records had to be kept up to date and you had your own ward rounds. In the beginning there was a lot to learn from the casualty and other sisters, but later in the year they were learning from you about routines and practices. When you got into a spot of trouble you could phone the GP's in charge of the hospital, but you didn't always get the help you needed and then had to follow your own instinct at your own discretion.

You came across all kinds of incidents, such as two policemen that had to transport a corpse to the mortuary in the back of the pickup. When they went over a bump in the road, they heard a moan and after a discussion between them they decided they couldn't take him to the mortuary and headed for the hospital with the corpse propped up between them as if he was still alive, where I had to confirm that he was indeed dead.

In serious cases you have to do everything possible to keep your casualties alive, but with the best will you sometimes saw patients die in front of your eyes. You then had to write a report on the presentation, what you did and the sequence of events. In this case the patient needed a forensic autopsy done by an appointed doctor. This was followed by giving evidence so you needed to be clear and without doubt if you didn't want to be torn apart by the lawyers and made to believe you were the one that killed the patient.

With emergencies you were on your own and you had to resuscitate the patients to the best of your ability, then inform the general practitioner on duty and sometimes you needed to accompany the patient to the next larger hospital 60 miles away in Pretoria to hand over the patient yourself. The GP then took over your duty at casualty.

On your return you needed to continue seeing patients. It wasn't a game and you had to remain responsible for everything that you did or didn't do.

In another case a son almost killed his own father for the sake of a blanket in the winter. He was stabbed in the neck and had to go to Pretoria.

You had to keep your own statistics and if events didn't happen to expectation, you needed to take your own steps to improve your system, such as better isolation of maternity cases and the paediatric ward, without going overboard.

Industrial cases were usually private (Injuries on duty) and then you could expect remuneration for your initial service, before you handed the patient over to the GP.

With interviews and negotiations at the end of your internship, you could choose which private practice you wanted to join before you started your proper career.

In preparation for my general practice I acquired a 220 Mercedes out of the box. My first brand new car.

With general practise you commenced another series of firsts and if your patients told you it was the first time they'd seen a doctor, you had to resist the temptation of telling them they were your first patient.

My First Private Practice.

The practice I joined was a solo practice, with me as the second partner and I was on alternative nights and alternative weekends. I learnt here to extract teeth and quite soon I was approached by the town's lawyer to extract one of his teeth. He did not want local anaesthetic as he had primed himself with alcohol before his visit. It was difficult to find out what his story was and I quickly gathered what the situation was – after examination I noticed that his tooth was beyond repair. The dental board rule was that if there wasn't a dentist available within 50 miles, you could stand in as a dentist.

One weekend I was presented with a maternity emergency and with no ambulance available I had to make arrangements for a caesarean section 100 miles away. It was a hand before the head presentation, with no way I could push it back. With her sedated I had to take her in my own car on unknown gravel roads at night, through mountain passes, neither of which I had done before.

With her on my back seat in my brand new yellow 220 Mercedes, I had to leave the town's patients to their own mercies and take the road. On the gravel road and turns I started going slower and slower until the patient started screaming and I had to go faster again. I arrived at the neighbouring town 3 hours later and handed the patient over, ready to assist. The end of the story was that mother and baby were well.

At 0600 hours the next morning, when I set off on my own, with my eyes wanting to close, it started snowing, creating a hypnotic kaleidoscopic effect. The snow appeared to be creating a funnel with the snowflakes departing in different directions and the side of the road becoming less and less visible due to the snow that had fallen already. I arrived home in Barkley East three hours later and after one hours sleep I was back on duty again to see everyone that needed my attention.

Due to a misunderstanding and mutual mistrust, matters did not work out with my partner. The receptionist cried that I accused her of taking the petty cash from the tin. I was entitled to half of it and it was all I had to live on before the accounts were paid. (Sometimes the patients only paid yearly at the end of the harvest.) It later transpired that she had taken more than half the petty cash (hot cash) for years prior to that.

I gave my wife three choices of where she wants to settle and where I could go to try and get a job in a hospital. She chose Durban and 2 days later I arrived at Addington Hospital, saw the superintendent and I had work again. I chose a medicine department in order to spice up my medical knowledge.

I looked for homes, chose a place in the Bluff and signed on the dotted line.

We went back to Barkley East to collect the furniture and arrange transport and went back to Durban again.

I only found out later that Merebank, where my grandmother had been held in the concentration camp and my great grandmother died, was close to the Bluff in Durban.

My maternal grandfather had been on the other end of town in the Umbilo concentration camp, just before you reach Durban North. I stayed in the Bluff for 18 months, working in Addington, where I had worked 5 years previously as a student.

THE BLUFF IN DURBAN
AND DURBAN NORTH

The Bluff was my domicile for 18 months. With my stand in Erasmusrand, Pretoria, sold, I could get a loan to buy the house in the Bluff. One of the first things I did was to landscape the rear garden to my taste. It was divided into two terraces with even ground, which I changed into one terrace on a slight slope from the kitchen to the rear end of the garden.

At the one end, in the corner, I built a braai in a sunken circle, with a chimney and a chimney valve. With the valve open the draught was so strong that the sparks flew 25 foot into the air. It also had an adjustable grill, that could flip to turn it. I learnt from my Dad as tradesman to design my own patent and constructed it. Sometimes it was copied, but that never worried me as it was for my own use. At that point in time I did not have a welding machine and assembled everything with nuts and bolts.

My play area was Brighton strand. I remember that I once tried surfing. With me in the water I waited for a nice big breaker, unfortunately by the time I was ready it was the last one, close to the beach and I nose-dived onto the sand of the beach, with my stomach on the other end. After one of these episodes I felt a cool breeze on my backside and gathered my swimming trunk had given notice, with the seam burst open. With the surfboard held behind me, protecting my modesty, I reached my beach towel.

On another occasion I decided to go out with the rip tide and approach the beach from way behind and just as I made good progress, the life guard came to "rescue" me.

I decided then that unless I got coaching, it would be best to stop my attempts and I never had the opportunity to learn after that.

It was also in the Bluff that my future ex-wife was one of the last people to watch a whale slaughter.

I gathered that all my overtime work all went towards paying for my Mercedes and if I got rid of it, I wouldn't have to do casualty. Instead I bought 2 small cars, one for my wife as she wanted to work and one for me. During my student years and again my future ex-wife regularly worked "overtime".

After my additional experience in medicine and paediatrics, I was approached to acquire a private practice from a doctor who developed cancer and had to retire. After an interview and working my notice, I was ready to start my own solo practice. I decided to upgrade my domicile and sold the place in the Bluff at a profit after my landscaping, and then bought a place in Durban North. The practice itself was in Durdoc centre in the middle of town and was mainly a town practice with patients from the town itself. The plan was to keep all those patients and in addition to accept new patients on a route between Durban North and town.

I realised soon enough that to buy a practice from a dying senior doctor that I had bought a dying practice. With each patient that died my practice grew smaller and the new younger patients that joined the practice did not get ill that often. I held my own but my take home income did not grow that much with inflation, despite fee increases.

At a stage I decided to take up an appointment as Railway doctor and made a vow not to treat them any different than my own private patients. What was clear to me was how neglected the health of these people were. Due to my approach I was quickly overwhelmed with work and I often made a diagnosis of serious conditions. Soon my private patients objected and I had to differentiate by splitting my times to see both groups.

I shared my rooms with a doctor from Scotland, and his father and got quite a lot of help from him. His first hint was when he pointed out to me that I was in competition with my own receptionist, who was a trained nurse and who gave my patients help and advice instead of referring them to me. This was acceptable in a hospital setup, but not a private practice.

A practice is also a business and the bigger your overheads were, the less you could take home. I was now in a position where I had to fire her and used the excuse that my future ex-wife would be standing in as receptionist, while at the same time I had to interview her replacement candidates. At last she left my employment. I then appointed a receptionist with no medical knowledge, but with secretarial qualifications.

She quickly established a good understanding of my routine and she knew my route and knew where she could fit patients in and informed me of serious cases and could re-organise my appointments. She also was able to give me a hint what the appointments were about. We were in contact with a pager system and once she told me about a funny patient which stormed into the room, started moaning and rolling about on the floor. It didn't take me much imagination to gather that he most likely had renal colic and I had to leave my house rounds to get to the room as quickly as possible to give him pain relief, while she organised a bed in hospital. I ordered an ambulance and got him a consultation with a urologist to take over his case.

On another occasion there was a patient who became white in his face, with a pain in his groin, collapsing on his garage floor. This was one of the most urgent cases I had. While I raced there I immediately realised that he most likely had a raptured aortic aneurism and when I got there he barely had any pulse. I accompanied him in the ambulance and started giving him intravenous fluids and in hospital started giving him unmatched group O negative blood followed by serum, until I could get matched blood. I asked the ward sister to get hold of a vascular surgeon immediately, explaining the nature of the emergency, while I continued monitoring his progress. He started responding and I was worried that the surgeon might think I had called him in vain, but he soon caught on when he rapidly deteriorated again. The practice was, that when you referred a patient to a surgeon, you assisted at the operation. In that way you knew the capability of your specific surgeon and who you could rely on with future referrals.

As it happened there was a surgeon on his rounds in the hospital and he contacted a vascular surgeon who also came to see the patient. An emergency theatre was booked and before long we were all in theatre. One of the complications in this case was that he had congenital telangiectasis in his nose with high blood pressure and had frequent nose bleeds and was chronically anaemic.

With a solo practice you are constantly on duty night and day and on call. With a flu epidemic you had your chance to gain cases from other doctors who were ill themselves, to make up for all your quiet times, until you become ill yourself. Such an epidemic usually lasted a month but this time it was a triple epidemic and no sooner a patient recovered, they became ill again, lengthening the time of the epidemic.

One story I heard was of the hypochondriac old lady that was referred to a specialist and her doctor handed her the referral letter to the specialist. She was curious to see what the doctor wrote and steamed the envelope open and inside she saw the note that simply said "Fat goose, pluck well". That always reminded me not to give referral letters to patients, but to ensure that it got posted. Not that I ever wrote such notes.

In general practice you learnt a lot about new medicines from the pharmaceutical representatives, but you needed to remain on your guard for false claims from rogue companies.

Every now and then there were symposiums organised by one or more pharmaceutical firms and sponsored by more than one firm. You also had continual education with lectures, also sponsored by pharmaceutical firms. You had the opportunity to mix with your colleagues and get to know them. It was an essential part of general practice. Nowadays you need to register for symposia and it costs you a small fortune.

There were two kinds of practices: the "kill or cure" where few referrals took place and the "Penicillin and aspro" groups that referred anything that they couldn't cure with penicillin and aspro, and with some of them in between. I tried to follow an in between approach.

I had a loose association with a group of other practitioners where they saw your patients and sent out the accounts themselves but with the understanding they didn't take your patients over. One of the only ways I could get a break was to take a Friday and Monday of with the weekend in between once a month. For longer breaks to see the family in Transvaal, you took two weekends off with the week in between.

Your receptionist then took time off simultaneously to give her a break. If your receptionist wanted to take time off for her own purposes, she organised a replacement herself.

My future ex-wife didn't just work, she still worked overtime for her own reasons, saying that her firm needed her. As I had only 50 percent viable sperm count we made an agreement that she should not have donor sperm, and that we would prefer to adopt a child, who wasn't related to either of us. It was before the days of selective in vitro fertilisation and we applied for adoption, but after 7 years of marriage my daughter was born with typical Boshoff features compared to my nieces. My ex-wife had anti serum with our daughter's birth. My ex-wife had been blood group O, Rh negative and my daughter had been blood group A, Rhesus negative, which gave me a 12.5% chance of being the biological father.

Three and a half years later we moved back to the Transvaal to work for the mine company, the same company that made my rooms unaffordable. If you can't beat them, join them. Two years later our adoption came through and rather than waiting a full seven years we decided to carry on with the adoption. The advantage of working for the mine company was that I could build up a pension and have regular holidays.

Before we left Durban, I just want to mention that it became a family gathering place for my brothers to have a free holiday. At times I still worked while they were having a holiday and matters did not always run according to plan. If you were the only one having to remain sober, you started seeing everything in a different light. When I could party along them it ran much more smoothly. It was here that our five brothers all met together for the last time, before each started dispersing in different directions.

With these reunions we could compare notes by comparing assets and debts and our income per hour from the time we started working, until one of my younger brothers commented "We are all in the shit, it is only the depth that varies". Only my brother just younger than me and I, completed a university degree – the others started working soon after matric.

My choice to became a doctor rested on the choice whether I wanted to work with people or things. I couldn't work with people as a hobby but I could still work with things as a hobby, but my brother who wanted to work with things ended up working with people. He measured his success in how much money he could sign on for.

In Durban I built up a whole collection of orchids which I grew under shade in the corner of my garden (In a shade house). I was quite successful flowering my orchids with the help of a sprinkler system and 2 weekly feeds and also started an orchid judging course to learn even more about orchids. I unfortunately left Durban before I could complete the course.

I also had an interest in astronomy and built my own telescope by grinding my own hollow mirror and constructing the rest of the telescope. I joined the astronomical society and learned the difference between astronomy and astrology. My ultimate dream was to sail the world on my own seagoing yacht so my aim was to learn the stars for astronavigation and to become self-sufficient. I also bought a metal lathe which helped me in completing the telescope. I also did the electronics for my telescope, with the help of one of the members of the society. I met Patrick Moore and Steven Hawkins before the latter became wheelchair bound and at that time he could move around in crutches. I listened to him talking about black holes and the horizon event with head nodding, while I hadn't had the foggiest idea what he was talking about. I was quite certain I wasn't the only one, I just didn't admit it to anyone.

I built my 8inch telescope in my workroom on a 44 gelling drum, half filled with water to give it weight. I ground the lens with graded carborundum grit in increasing steps of fineness until I got to polishing it with rouge and a pitch lap on a disc of wood. It took several months doing it part time, whenever I had time and/or motivation. There were plenty of books to help with the project. My telescope was a Newtonian with the eyepiece at the upper end, but still in reach as it was a $1/8^{th}$ focal ratio and ended up with an accuracy of $1/8^{th}$ the wavelength of light, which was good. With my lathe the task was to cut a 359 tooth gear out of a brass disc by skipping teeth, correcting and counter correcting accumulative errors as it wasn't a natural number to cut. The telescope was driven by a worm gear, with an electronic speed control that worked off a 12 Volt car battery. The treat was testing it out and looking at stars and moon craters of known distances apart so that I could measure the magnification and definition. It had 2 clutches in 2 axes with the telescope set up to the celestial south pole. (In South Africa – in the UK you would set it up to the celestial North pole). Each axis had a disc divided and marked in 360 sections. You could see the red dot of Jupiter and the rings of Saturn with most of its moons. My telescope was wieldy but optically it compared well with the shop bought ones. Half the fun was in building it yourself. I got rid of my learned barbarian status.

While in Durban I also visited Champagne castle in the Drakensberg, with the orchid society, to take photographs of the natural terrestrial orchids. You were able to spot most of them by going in the group, who knew where the different locations were.

While in Durban we visited the Hluhluwe game reserve, Midmar nature park and the Oribi gorge valley and even went to Richards Bay for a weekend.

Our neighbours had a swimming pool and my daughter learnt to swim there. I built her a pedal cart out of old washing machine plates, pop-riveted together – unfortunately this was too heavy for her but my sons later made good use of it until my future ex-wife annihilated it with our pickup on the small holding in Klerksdorp.

My receptionist had gone on holiday and was involved in a car crash, her boyfriend unfortunately lost his life. I had to employ a new receptionist. It was almost like starting with a new practice and combined with all the other considerations. The economy was weak and with the attraction of doing my own operations in the goldmines, I made the decision to sell up and leave Durban for Klerksdorp. The actual hospital was in Orkney, close to Klerksdorp.

After I had found someone to take over the practise I moved out of Durban. A lot of my patients saw me go with regret and I received their good wishes. Durban taught me to speak better English and strengthened my prospects later on. In Klerksdorp I was destined to move three times.

NESERHOF, KLERKSDORP

My first house was in Klerksdorp, Neserhof as there wasn't anything available in Orkney immediately. I acquired a glasshouse for my orchids, installed a second hand air conditioner with a thermostat, and lined it with shade cloth which was when my DIY expertise failed me. A month later we were awakened by frantic knocking on the front door. I saw that everything was nice and pink, but when I opened the curtains, I saw the greenhouse was on fire – fortunately away from the house. I immediately pulled out the plug supplying the greenhouse, slipped out the side door and hosed everything down. When I came back in the house the knocking continued and there was a woman telling me the greenhouse was on fire. I apologised for keeping her waiting and said we had already extinguished it and thanked her for her concern. The problem was that the thermostat wasn't rated for the air conditioner (It should have had a relay switch) It worked by cutting out when the circuit overheated. I thought it was a very sensitive thermostat, until it didn't work anymore and caused a short circuit.

I was in Neserhof, Klerksdorp for barely 15 months, when we were notified by the social workers that they had a son for us and we needed to go and fetch him. The hospital superintendent was very understanding and granted me immediate three days leave and off we went back to Durban to fetch our son.

Due to my diagnosis with sub fertility and not cancelling the adoption application when my daughter was born, we decided it would be better to go ahead with the adoption, rather than waiting another 7 years before we had another child. My daughter was then 5 years old and we didn't want her to be a single child.

ORKNEY, KLERKSDORP

After 18 months in Neserhof we had to move to Orkney because it was closer to Hospital, where I was on call. It would save me some time in the mornings and I was back half an hour earlier in the evenings and could go home during lunch breaks. It was here where I learned about Patterson ratings, which determined what size carpet you could have in your house. Also if you were entitled, or not, to a swimming pool, if there was one, they would fill it in so that you didn't exceed your Patterson rating. The higher up you were on the Patterson scale, the closer in the "A" streets you move. We were moved into **B**acon Road which wasn't bad, and we could have a full carpet in the dining room, but no swimming pool,

From Klerksdorp and Orkney we could go to Pretoria or Roodepoort on a long weekend. With holiday breaks we could drive anywhere, with so much more time available in one go we could visit new places, sometimes with my brothers or on our own.

WILKOPPIES, KLERKSDORP

Nice wasn't nice anymore as you never felt you were away from work and all the regulations due to Patterson ratings. You were issued a car from the mine company, also according to Patterson rating. Basically you couldn't set your own priorities and you got called out at the drop of a hat. You were also off the property ladder.

With the 15 golden Kruger rand that I had bought from the proceeds of selling my house in Durban North, in my pocket, I set off to a money trader with trepidation and anxiety, should I get ambushed. There I had them converted into paper money which I deposited in my bank account. (It was one month before the gold price dived sharply.)

We could now afford to buy a five-acre smallholding in Klerksdorp with a windmill and a few out buildings.

It bordered on a residential area but still peri-urban. We later concluded that it was originally a garage, that had been converted into a house by adding on 2 front rooms, as one of the inside walls was a double wall. The original garage formed a bedroom and kitchen with a bathroom on the outside and then with the 2 front rooms added. It had a dining room and sitting room. With even further expansion another room was added as a bedroom. Thus a 3-stage dwelling ending up with 2 bedrooms one bathroom, one kitchen, dining room and a lounge. The outside buildings consisted of a separate granny flat with 2 bedrooms, connected to the main house by an arch, which made it a legal extension. Apart from this was a garage with servant quarters, which was converted into working rooms and a lean-to garage was added.

Further back two servant quarters were added and behind that was the windmill and dam. A real farming tramp situation. But it was all mine and it could only be improved. This later proved to be more difficult and costly than I anticipated.

This was the only time in my life that I had 3 vehicles, the company Peugeot 504, an Audi 1600 and an old Ranchero pickup, which we needed for transporting a variety of items. I soon acquired 4 German Marino ewes and a ram as well as a Guernsey cow. My daughter's mates arrived one day with a donkey and seemed to enjoy it, so I looked out for a horse and got hold of a neglected "thoroughbred" which we brought back from the brink. My daughter then learnt to ride horses and a bit of dressage on a neighbouring smallholding. Meanwhile our servant "broke" the horse in and I got a jumping saddle with jodhpurs and boots for my daughter. She was also doing ballet classes. The horse got named "Lady" and my daughter got teased with the nickname, "Merrie" for mare.

To further the "farming" we acquired some chicks to rear for slaughter and got hold of a stunner, bleeding through and a de-feathering apparatus. I sheared my own sheep with a hand shearer but due to lack of knowhow the wool got spoilt and I couldn't use it. I had in mind to comb it and spin it, but I not ever got that far.

When the farm-help became hungover, I had to milk the cow myself. In the end she stopped giving milk and I asked a farmer friend to get her covered with his bull. He told me she didn't take and would have to be slaughtered. I had to tell my family she had to be slaughtered, but it later transpired that she miscarried and started lactating. I had to now lie her alive again and bring her back home again. She gave 3 to 4 gallon of milk per day. Some of the milk I sold privately, until they heard of chlamydia. I had her milk tested for bovine TB, but she was clear. The excess milk was sold to the ice cream factory at a song for them.

Each season I prepared my soil with a petrol rotavator and planted mealies and had a good harvest for 2 years.

We had plenty of water from the windmill and dam until one of the neighbours sank a borehole with an electric pump and watered his lawn day and night, with the result that my waterhole dried up. This however coincided with a drought and one of my mature Camelthorn trees which were drought resistant died 2 years later due to the low water table, caused by the drought and the exploitation of my neighbour with his pump.

The whole idea of the small holding was an exercise in self-sufficiency and to raise my children to such an existence, so that they knew that milk came from the teats of cows and that meat came from slaughtered animals. They could also have an idea what was entailed to bring to fruition. I encouraged them to participate without forcing them but ended up doing most of the work myself when I was not at the hospital.

Throughout my medical career I strived to do things, rather than theorising. I learned to do Obstetrics during my houseman year and later. In Vaal Reefs I learned to do caesarean sections. I was also taught to do plating of long bones and ankles by a qualified orthopaedic surgeon, who was a perfectionist. I also experienced what to do when examining abdomens after knife stab wounds. We took turns from early on to do the anaesthetics, which included local blocks and spinals. With all this we became experts in resuscitations.

My future ex-wife in spite of all the smallholding activity decided to go back to work again and to work overtime again. Two years after my adopted son's arrival she got pregnant again. After this confinement she didn't need anti-serum, meaning that the baby couldn't be mine, as she was blood group O Rh negative and I was blood group A Rh positive. Blood group A and Rh+ is dominant over blood group O and Rh-. I decided at the time I didn't want to get divorced and lose everything I'd struggled to achieve and decided to "adopt" him as my own.

The problem was that I couldn't tell him I was not his biological father as that would spell divorce.

MY AEROPLANE

Before I come to the narration of Kleinzee I would just like to tell you about my aeroplane as it was one of my childhood dreams to fly my own plane. (With my dream to sail the world still lying dormant in the back ground).

I gathered that it would not be impossible to learn to fly. I could spread the cost and there was an instructor at hand. I went to see him and had a good conversation, had an induction flight, bought the books and committed myself to training. At this stage I had lost some of the daring of my youth, but he assured me everything would be OK.

I started the flying lessons in a Cessna 150 and after 12 hours flying I was ready for my first solo flight. Not looking at the empty seat next to me, everything went to plan as in the training flights and I made a perfect landing. With my 2nd solo flight I was more at ease and started looking around me and noticed the empty seat next to me and it dawned on me I was truly on my own. It was an askew approach and I landed harder than anticipated, but still safely. Thereafter I was taken through all the scenarios of engine failure and emergency landings and the various different manoeuvres to learn in preparation of my final test flight and examinations. He said that he flew by "IFR" (normally "Instrument flight rules"), but he took it to mean "I follow roads" or railroads. My instructor always asked me what I was afraid of – at 5,000 feet above ground there is plenty of time to decide what to do if anything goes wrong. My reply was that I was afraid of dying before the time I hit the ground. At last I'd done my examinations and was ready for my test flight.

As part of the pre final qualification, I had to complete a triangle to 2 towns, with handing in a flight plan. Klerksdorp to Venterstad, to Lichtenburg and back to Klerksdorp. It was an exercise of dead reckoning combined with identifying landmarks and beacons. (Not forgetting the roads) The flight plan included times, directions and speed and wasn't too difficult to accomplish. With previous flights you could remember and recognised the different towns from the air and follow your progress on your map. It was also important to watch the weather and forecasts. It wasn't too difficult and your local knowledge of the river courses and identifiable beacons, as well as which roads were tarred and which were not, was a big help. You also had to know the location of the different alternative airports and landing places in case of difficulties.

I would have to do my future flights in a hired plane and did a conversion to a Cessna 172 at Lanseria. It's stalling behaviour was much more gentle than in the Cessna 150.

Then I heard of an opportunity to acquire a half share in a Piper Cherokee 160, It was a 4 ½ seater aeroplane and low wing. You could not see the ground sideways unless you banked sharply, you could only see obliquely to the front and ahead. Another conversion was done.

One of my first flights was from Klerksdorp to Lanseria for an aircraft service. My instructor was accompanying me in another aircraft with a predetermined plan on how we would fly and how we flew in relation to each other. We were also in radio contact. Approaching the Rand there was a smoke and smog blanket that hung over the whole area, which extended pretty high into the air. He was to fly ahead and I had to follow him. He pointed out all the beacons and told me what direction and height to fly. The landing was quite surprising in that it was on a downhill slope and you kept on taxying forever.

My second flight was on my own with my family to Rustenburg. My second youngest brother was staying there and worked for Sun City. I worked out my flight plan, looked at the weather and worked out that I basically had to follow the road along the mountain pass, but at a safe height to compensate for up and down draughts. There was light rain as I flew at base of cloud level, enough to get me slightly worried, should it get any worse. The weather fortunately cleared and the skies opened up completely as per forecast.

I reached the pass and as soon I was through the pass I needed to throttle down to descend. I now had to identify my landmarks as on the map, without having seen them before. This I managed to do and landed with my family on board.

At the airport I had to phone my brother to come and fetch us. Fortunately, he didn't stay too far from the airport and was there in no time and we enjoyed our visit minus any drinks.

On the way back everything was the same but directions 180 degrees different. With the road in view towards the pass. I flew in my designated direction until I noticed a shallow mountain range ahead that was not on the map – I looked on my compass and noticed that I was 30 degrees off course and when I looked at my Gyro again I realised that I hadn't reset my gyro before taking off. I overcorrected my course by 60 degrees to get back on the track, I should have been on. I frantically looked for familiar beacons and the road from Rustenburg to Ventersdorp and Klerksdorp, annoyed with myself for making such an error. I started to pick up my landmarks and changed course to what it should have been in the first instance. We arrived safely in Klerksdorp airport.

On another occasion I decided to fly to Bloemfontein to visit friends of ours. The weather was favourable and filled with fuel and everything else checked (Including the gyro), the correct charts and flight plan worked out we set off. From the air the hills seemed completely flat and everything seemed the same, making identifying the beacons crucial. We reached Bloemfontein without any hiccups and I went through all the radio procedures and landed. I phoned our friends to pick us up. This was Saturday late morning. The same afternoon the clouds started accumulating and I said to my future ex-wife, we had better head back. "No", she said "we had only just arrived". Later in the afternoon it started raining and Sunday when we had planned to fly back it was still raining. It eased a bit on Sunday morning, but with a low cloud base. I phoned the airport and they confirmed that the cloud base was too low for small private aircraft. Thus we had to wait for Monday and notify the Hospital that I was stuck in Bloemfontein. This confirmed the saying of flying small planes "If you have time to spare, fly by air". From house to house driving by car had to be compared with house to airport, airplane out of hangar airport to airport, getting a lift to destination and you didn't really save time on distances shorter than 100 miles.

On Monday the clouds remained low and with lightning on all sides there was no chance of flying - we would have to make our own way. Our friends took us to just outside the town and we started to hitch-hike. Luckily we were picked up quite quickly. It was 1976 when South Africa was still tame and our benefactors took us all the way home.

The Wednesday after that the weather was favourable and by swapping duties, I got off early and we drove by car to Bloemfontein – after 20 minutes of driving I felt for my plane keys and they weren't there – I'd left them at home. I had to turn back again and I redid my sums and now instead of having plenty of time we are ending up on a tight squeeze – we lost 40 minutes at least. At Bloemfontein I notified them that I was flying back to Klerksdorp and left. I told my future ex-wife to look for me at each airport, starting two airports away from home to see if I'd landed there. I am now flying on my own and can't really fly faster, but looking at my watch and the amount of light outside, I convinced myself that I would make it in time before sundown. I had Klerksdorp airstrip in sight and the more I descend the lower the sun got and with only a rim of sun showing, I landed as it finally disappeared. The adaptation from sunlight to dark took time on landing and I had to switch my landing lights on. I got on the ground just after the sun disappeared below the horizon. I managed to land safely, but there was no way I would have been able to make it if I'd had to do a flypast and try again. By the time I got to the hangar it was properly dark. In the summer in South Africa you don't get a dusk as in UK.

This episode led me to doing a night rating. During training you fly wearing a hood so that you can only see your instruments. My instructor challenged me to make a steep turn, while keeping my height and chased me to remain in strict limits, while turning the whole time. My instrument panel just went berserk turning round and round. He asked me to tilt up my hood. I had no sensation of turning – as far I was concerned I had been stationary and it was the earth beneath me that went crazy, spinning in front of me. The engine was screaming as we lost height and were out of control in a spiral dive. The instructor took over, throttled down and by opposite rudder and aileron he stopped the rotation and slowly pulled the plane up again. He applied throttle after we slowed down. I realised later that if he hadn't been in the plane with me, that I would have dived happily into the earth without a care in the world. It wasn't me it was the earth that misbehaved.

Meanwhile I started building on to the house to create a more modern home.

That would have a large sitting room. Behind that on the ground floor there was a large dining room and on top of that as a double storey there was a big room to be a Study and hobby room – behind that on the ground floor there was a large playroom and a side annexe connecting the playroom with the rest of the house. Off the passage there was a toilet and the new kitchen, which was also renovated. Further on there were a second bathroom and shower, the main bedroom with an en suite bathroom and 3 more bedrooms. 4 Bedrooms in all. The new portion had a flat Everite roof. I extended the old building and built the new walls myself.

It wasn't long after this that I got offered a promotion to senior medical officer but if I accepted I would have to transfer to Kleinzee. I now had to sell my share in the aeroplane, as I wouldn't be able to use my share and would still be liable to pay half the upkeep.

KLEINZEE

For anyone that hasn't heard of Kleinzee: – Kleinzee is the 2nd last town close to the sea, before you leave South Africa, going northwards towards Namibia. Why go to Kleinzee. The biggest attraction was to get a promotion. It is really an artificial town on the stamp of the mine company culture and again the street addresses were allocated in order of the Patterson rating. They had however done a lot to make it more acceptable for the people living there. As it was meant for workers there were no older people, except for visitors.

My first impression was from a company aircraft – then a King Air, with the result that I didn't really appreciate how isolated it really was. Water pipelines had been laid on from Springbok for the mining operation, leaving enough water to keep the whole town green. The Patterson rating was less obvious, but all the higher rating people were in one street, but with lesser levels of distinction. They did everything in their power to remove any obstacles – there were 2 religious denominations, a primary school, a hospital with an operating theatre, a rugby and soccer field, a cricket field, a golf course, sailing club, tennis and squash courts, a bridge club and a bowling green. There was also a recreation hall with a bar, a farm, a general store, off license and a bank. You could even get your driving licence with municipality officials visiting the town.

The farm had a visiting veterinary surgeon and people with pets or horses could attend a clinic. At the hospital there were visiting specialists who came once a month, by appointment. For serious cases there was the company aircraft that could fly people with medical referrals to Cape Town. Sometimes by twisting the arms of the doctors, some people went to see a specialist in order to do shopping as a bonus. Also a gavel club (Public speaking club). Later also a visiting psychologist.

The mine area was cordoned off and out of bounds except for workers but guarded with security gates and fences and random X-Ray screening for diamonds. If positive, the miscreant was taken to hospital, signed permission to be examined and one of the doctors had to do a rectal examination and fish out, usually a plastic bag that had been pushed up into the rectum. If it couldn't be retrieved this way, he was given a laxative and guarded by security until there was a result. This was washed and sieved by the security services.

One story that got told repeatedly was that one of the miners came to the security gate with a wheelbarrow each day filled with gravel. Despite being searched daily the security could never find anything. When the miner retired he bought a small farm and one of the retired security blokes went to see him. When asked what he'd been doing because they knew he had been up to mischief. Easy, he said, "I was stealing the wheelbarrows." The whole town was guarded by security gates and there were only two roads leading in and out of town.

With all this information I could not object and with the proviso that I got the house of the previous medical officer that had left, I accepted the post.

Now I had to sort out the house on the smallholding. I had to complete the rest of the alterations in utmost haste so that the house could be rented out and get rid of all my animals with exception of the dogs.

The company car's usage period had expired and I could buy it and resell it privately, together with the Ford Ranchero pickup.

I retained an old VW combi and the Audi and left early morning from Klerksdorp with two vehicles. When I got to Kleinzee, I would be entitled to a new company car.

My future ex-wife drove the Audi and followed me in the VW combi as that was the least reliable vehicle. I had to transport everything that the removal van could not take. We stopped every 3 hours to fill up the cars and have comfort breaks. After replenishments and stretching our legs we carried on with the journey. The cars behaved and we arrived in Kleinzee by late afternoon. The last 50 km was a gravel road. We went through security, got the house keys and were met and welcomed by someone from personnel. We now had to wait for our removal lorry. This arrived a few hours later and we could move in.

The first priority was to get the beds ready, as no one was hungry due to all the snacks we'd had during travel. One wheel came off the main bed with the move and it wasn't usable. Armed with my self-sufficiency, I just had to weld it back on. I managed to find my welding machine and welding rods, but couldn't find my welding helmet anywhere. I remembered the personnel manager planned to build a steel boat and lived only two houses away from me. I asked him if I could borrow his welding helmet, which he couldn't lend me as he hasn't got one yet. He was so greatly amused that a doctor would want to borrow a welding helmet that he didn't forget about it up to my last day in Kleinzee. I just had to open up all the boxes until I found my helmet. I did the necessary welding repairs and we could go to bed.

I had a few days to settle in and soon got used to the new routine. My first extra mural activity was the golf course and I settled between the beginners. My handicap was golf itself with hook shots and chasing rabbits off the field. Later I did improve, but I remained a beginner. The wind in Kleinzee did not improve matters.

Although I worked for the mine company, the mine was operated by a subsidiary and when I visited the recreation club I was amused by a T-shirt reading "I am here for de(the) Beers"

One of the sayings in Kleinzee was that you could drink as much as you like, provided you didn't get drunk.

There were regular mine functions and as medical practitioners, you were invited to them all. They told me about one of the light green workers who still stood upright talking to the manager one moment and the next he was flat on his face. He had to be carried out and only woke up the next morning.

I made friends with the farm manager, as he was a friend of one of my future ex-wife's uncles, who were involved with animal husbandry and farming activities. I learned to make proper "potjiekos" in all its varieties, also how to make ash bread. I also learned about the flora, which plants you could utilise in the veld for toilet uses, what was edible etc.

Another adage was "In Namaqualand if you get an urge to do something, you take a walk into the veld and look for a stone on which you can sit, then you wait for the urge to pass over."

Cray fishing was another activity – it was not just about snorkelling, you had to know what sort of places the crayfish hid and where on the coast the best places were.

The horse riding was meant for my daughter and I soon learned what that meant especially when she started going to high school in the Paarl. I had to go and feed the horse and keep exercising it, with the result that I started horse riding myself. Nothing was nicer than going for a ride into the veld if it was flowering time and there were flowers everywhere. We were in Namaqualand for 2 years when the Buffels river came down in flood for the first time in 12 years (Normally a dry bed.)

Buffels river in flood.

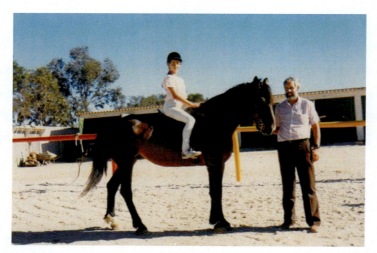

My daughter, with some friends of her friends tried to go through the river on horseback
after the flood subsided, but before the water was gone, but her horse didn't want to
know. His name was "Jasper" a Basutho pony and very calm, except near water.

My daughter went for a ride at the seaside and her horse slipped and threw her off, then fell
on top of her head, with her face in the water. Luckily her horse got up and the situation didn't
get any worse, but she had a big fright. Later with a lot of patience she taught her horse to

jump over a 6" high beam. Horse riding was a family event and we had a Gymkhana as well with good memories.

I also tried Squash – with the good life and all the parties, I'd put on excessive weight and decided to learn to play squash with my farmer friend. We matched each other well and could work up a good sweat.

The Gavel club came in good stead later in Cape Town, when I joined the Rotarians.

Bowls also provided good competition. I measured up well against a man from the geological department at a yearend solo competition and I won a small trophy.

A scuba diving club was created as there was enough interest to get it going. We exercised in the town's swimming pool, followed by a week's intensive course in Gordons Bay. You had to provide your own wetsuit, weight belt, flippers and diving goggles. It was my birthday and unfortunately the blokes enticed me to drink chasers with pips in and I got more intoxicated than was good for me, with the result that I had to redo the test. (I later realised that it was to do me in, rather than me conforming to their pleasures, what the English call buggering.)

It was here I first saw what it really was to throw a moony. A traffic warden stopped them and asked them "what their case was to sit with their arses out of the window". It was due to eating humble pie and his sense of humour that we were let go. (I did not take part as I was under the weather.)

Wind Surfing was also one of the activities that was new to me. At Kleinzee there was an artificial lagoon filled with sea water. When it was getting too saline and started crystallizing salt, they'd acquired a condemned working pump from the mine, so they could pump water in and then out again. That way they got it back to seawater salinity again.

The wind over the lagoon at the best of time was blowing pretty strong. I was determined to stay on top of my surf board. I had my wet suit on (essential against the cold water) and my diving boots that had a tight grip on the surf board, but the wind finally blew me off. My feet retained their grip and I twisted my left knee through 90 degrees before I landed in the water with a pain in my knee. I immediately realised I have done some damage and with the help of the board I hobbled to the edge and the mooring jetty. I managed to put my board away and got into the car. I watched my knee blowing up as it warmed up in the car. I was completely on my own and eventually got my car in 2nd gear and slowly made my way to town, 3 km away. The gate guard, fortunately recognised me and I got through the gate without stopping. When I got home there was no one there and I continued to the hospital where one of the sisters helped me to put a Robert Jones bandage on, reinforced with a slab of plaster of Paris and gave me a pair of crutches.

I was the only doctor left in town out of 3 doctors, over that weekend with one on leave and another one off duty. On the Monday I made an appointment to see an orthopaedic surgeon in Cape Town, the following week and arranged a place on the company plane. The damage was worse than I had anticipated as I had a torn posterior cruciate ligament, a torn medial meniscus and a torn medial collateral ligament. I was operated on straight away. I was in a plaster of Paris for 8 weeks and the same time in an active splint before my knee recovered, but it was the end of my squash and windsurfing.

One of my previous colleagues discovered a family in a neighbouring town with a high prevalence of cancer, that only appeared in the males. After I found the previous records, I started reading up. (There wasn't internet as we know it today, neither was there digital photography or text file – You could connect to database data and download it by telephone line if you had a program to read it, e.g. share prices.) I first contacted the colon surgery department in Cape Town who put me in contact with the Genetic department, who was previously involved with the family. The surgical team, with the genetic team were invited to visit us to see our patients, that were overdue for a follow up, rather than waiting for problems to arise before referral. Once these patients presented with cancer it was only a question of a few months before they died.

The genetic guru informed me of a family in America, but this involved the females as well. We realised that we had a research bias, in that the company only attended to the male workers and we didn't know anything about the wives of the workers or their dependants. We all went to the neighbouring town to gain genetic and genealogical information to build a family tree, by talking to the elders in the community.

There were originally 3 brothers of the surname involved – For confidentiality I will name them "Pompies" - and who their immediate relatives were. We got permission from the mine company to attend to the women in this family with an understanding that no discrimination would be directed against this family on grounds of their surname and we decided to first compile a complete tree of all the "Pompies" family and whenever I saw any "Pompies" patients, I recorded their family ties and soon had a big family tree. All the patients that had a history of bowel problems were highlighted to see what part of the family tree they occupied.

It brought me in conflict with the rest of my colleagues as it was time consuming, but I persisted. (Later I also realised that it caused professional jealousy, despite me claiming no credit in the project.)

In the end the geneticists, after taking blood from everyone involved, did discover an indirect marker gene to point out the ones most at risk. This was accompanied by population education to get their co-operation. We could now focus our attentions on the people most at risk, to save both time and money, and spare the rest of the population the anxiety of being at risk. Long after I left the mine company, I received mention in an article by their "Outreach" publication.

With a psychologist visiting the hospital my future ex-wife and I attended as well and she advised us to divorce, which neither of us wanted to do at that stage.

The end of this story was that with my deafness as reason for disability, I applied for a medical pension.

GROWING UP EVENTUALLY

With my pension money I could buy a house in Bellville, Cape Town and had enough money left to buy the hull of a 39ft sailing boat and try to fulfil my ultimate dream. I got rid of my toxic debt and sold my small holding with brand new house, in which I have barely lived myself in completed form. The mine in Stilfontein sold all their houses to their workers, subsequently closed the mine, leaving their workers in houses that they now couldn't afford as they'd now lost their jobs as well. The result was that the whole area in Klerksdorp was now flooded with cheap houses and the whole housing market collapsed. It meant that all the money I'd spent on my house, including the deposit, went for the privilege to stay in the house up to the stage that I'd left it. (But having my house in Bellville, fully paid off, made up for it and left me without any further worries.) With the new South Africa at the door, people in 1994 were hesitant to live in the countryside and the writing was on the wall. The whole Cape was a relative safe bet, so good riddance to the smallholding and my old dreams. Now I had new dreams with a boat almost ready to escape to where-ever if I needed to.

I was permanently partially disabled due to my deafness and other disabilities, but with the mine company it was an all or nothing approach and I was on full medical pension, projected to retirement age, which meant that if I declared all my disabilities or worked part time, I could still work and have my pension. At Cape Provincial Administration I was good enough medically and academically to get employment at Somerset Hospital as GP-orthopaedic surgeon on the grounds of my experience. Here, in addition, I learned to do hip prosthesis insertions, Knowel pins and to deal with femoral fractures with Kuncher pins. Also femur neck fractures and knee plating for tibial plateau fractures with tibial pins and plating. All operations were planned ahead and properly written up post-operatively.

I had always put on plaster of Paris of my patients, as moulding the plasters were an important part of my treatment e.g. pretibial plaster of Paris and to ensure that the joint below and above the fracture is immobilised. Arm plasters were put on with the fingers still free to move to prevent disability. (We had disability assessment clinics, as the outcome of treatment was important to assess for compensation and for quality of treatment.)

I controlled and was in charge of the Orthopaedic Department under the guidance of an Orthopaedic surgeon.

I had a house officer under me for clerking and seeing to the everyday needs of the patients and to prepare them for operations. With my experience of theatre work and hospital administration, I was setting my own rules and targeted emergency surgery mainly. All my cases were discussed with Grootte Schuur Hospital Orthopaedic Department and I visited them with all my X rays for discussions and suggestions. I also managed more routine, minor cold cases.

I rotated after hour duties with casualty, so that I was off duty half the week and alternative weekends.

We had outpatient sessions as well and I remember a case of a work shy bloke who claimed his ankle was broken arriving in a wheelchair. Unbeknown to the sister I noticed there was no swelling or bruising and had seen his X-Rays before he came back in and as he came in I told him to "Stand up and walk, you are healed", which he did to the utter amazement of the sister. She just said "Hey, hey!" and rolled her eyes at me.

If any cases that were beyond my experience, I could refer them to Grootte Schuur. After a few years I choose my own boss to head my department in Somerset Hospital by creating a more senior post for a consultant from Grootte Schuur with motivation for such a post to reduce my responsibility. We now could do more operations at Somerset hospital and refer less patient to

Grootte Schuur and we had a bigger rotation and was now on duty 1 in 3 days and only every 3rd weekend.

While I was off duty, I could regularly go off sailing and did a course on the big "DAM". (Atlantic Ocean). I belonged to Royal Cape Yacht club and made plenty of new friends.

To try to solve my marriage problem, my future ex-wife and I went to see qualified hypnotherapists. We each had our own therapist.

Up to that stage I tried to solve all my problems with logic and I was always in control. Action – reaction and counter reaction. The better I got, the better my wife got. She actually just mirrored any arguments straight back at me and we got nowhere. She took over control of the children and did as she wanted with the result that I had withdrawn. We each started moving in our own direction. I lost her and my kids, but I still had some innings left with my kids.

At my first appointment with my psychologist she asked me what I expect from her and my reply was "That I want to be in control of myself and everyone around me" and especially that "she should help me to help myself". I read "Healing the child from within" and all it told me was that I had a problem but not what to do about it. I later realised it was just a reference for further discussion and communication.

What both my psychologist and I realised was that within one or two consultations she would be able to diagnose what my problem was and what I should do to overcome my problem, but unless I developed my own insights, it will be of no use to me.

With several sessions she hypnotised me and took me into regression and afterwards she gave me a tape recording to do my own self-hypnosis.

I realised that to get the most out of my sessions, I'd have to do my own homework and in this way I reached my insights one by one. The emphasis was on child abuse and one of my early insights was that I hadn't minded the abuse per se, but that I couldn't do without the love that I needed. (My parents also both had a problem, that was unresolved.)

I could remember that my Dad kicked us when we were bigger, but we ducked and ran away. We were laughing at him, when his knee gave way and he had to hobble until it slipped back in again.

With my mother the issue was that she gave all her attention to the younger children and ignored me. Possible sibling rivalry?

It was all made worse by the continual shouting between my father and mother and the liquor abuse – especially later on.

Eventually I also came to the insight that to control everyone around you only made yourself and the people around you unhappy, and that you needed to go with the flow without getting torn away by the current. "Live and let live". A psychology test revealed I was an INJF type personality. I learned the difference between self-assertion and aggression.

Eventually I realised was that I had choices to make and if my choice was not acceptable or compatible, I had the choice of leaving.

Breaking up wasn't what I wanted but there was no other way. My catharsis now began and with self-hypnosis and further psychological support, I overcame the cause of my unhappiness and started becoming more myself. (I had made peace with both my parents before they died.)

I lived in a separate part of the house to my family and came and went to suit myself.

At that time, I belonged to the Rotarian society and once a month you could bring a partner. I arrived each time with a different partner, sometimes very much younger than myself with the members jeering in envy. Altogether 5 or 6 partners until I actually got divorced and left for England.

The initial date for the divorce was set on my wedding anniversary day, but when I told my lawyer, she changed it to another date.

My choice was not to be on my own and I started looking around.

One of my dates was a lawyer and I could only imagine her taking me to court, should I try to kiss her against her will or worse. I told her that I was not ready for a new relationship and got the hell out of there.

The telephone operator at the hospital knew who each of my new flames were and where to contact me if my pager was out of reach in cases of emergency.

One of my girlfriends, after initially being approachable told me she wasn't hard-up, so she was off the score-card as well.

Before I left for the UK and after I was divorced, I stayed in a flat close to the hospital.

I frequented a 30+ social group and I met an English woman, who encouraged me to come to England and offered me a home base from where I could do locums in England. She was quite a few years older than me.

In converted money, I could earn more in England as a junior, than with my senior post in Somerset Hospital and seeing that my aim was to get my boat on the water, I accepted the locum post. At this stage R6 = £1.

I also acquired a small dwelling in a gated community close to Mountain view to live in at a later date, or to remain on the property ladder, which I could also let it out if I went to England. It was a small complex of 4 houses side by side and back to back with 1½ bedrooms, a bathroom with toilet, kitchen/dining room/ sitting room in one space. A small veranda with place for a braai and a separate communal garage.

It was completed but with the small deposit that I could afford, the letting out would not cover the back payments so that I'll have to subsidise it and there was no supervision on the renters. After a few months in England I stopped receiving rent and on letting my lawyer know, she investigated and reported there was children drawings all over the walls, I had to cut my losses and sell the property just to get rid of my obligation. A feeling of deja-vu from Klerksdorp. I was exploited and paid too much for the property in the first instance. Also changed politics in SA.

ENGLAND

I had and understanding with my ex, she got a fully paid house and I could leave my tools in her garage with my boat in her front garden, if I continue to pay for her psychotherapy sessions for a year. (The boat's keel stub was sunk into the ground – It was a 39ft sailing yacht). I also had to pay for my sons' courses in IT for a year as per divorce agreement.

I left South Africa in June 1996.

My children and ex came to see me off at the airport. My ex and I did not hate each other. We both realised that we had different ideals and needed space.

By leaving South Africa it would give me the opportunity to break away and as pioneer in a foreign land, give my children an open door for refuge if the politics didn't work out. The choice was in their hands. I had no other ties in South Africa, except my pension, which I could draw anywhere. I was self-sufficient and the world was my oyster. As I found out later with my genealogical research, I was actually closer to my roots in England than in South Africa and the ancestors of most people in England, came from Europe, only the other side of the English Channel. Even the English Royal family have ties all over Europe and Russia.

On arrival in England my english lady met me at the airport so I wouldn't land there, completely stranded and lost. My first locum appointment was in Bridgend, Mid Glamorgan for 2 weeks, before I went to North Allerton for 6 months. In Wales I learned that if I spelled my surname as "Bwshwff", they would pronounce my surname faultlessly as in Afrikaans.

The routine in A&E was completely different to what I expected and demanding. It included medical cases as well and the name of the department was misleading as barely half of the cases were emergencies. I would define an emergency as something that is a threat to life or could give rise to permanent disability, if not treated immediately. U.K. GP's on the other hand viewed anything that may require admission as not belonging in their consultation room as an emergency, even though they knew more about each patient's medical history than anyone else. There was not a direct route from the GP to the wards, unlike South Africa.

I was young enough at 53 to fit into a new routine and to do what was expected of me. Quite quickly the 2 weeks was over. I'd seen my english lady twice. She had a Jacuzzi bath and a nice big double bed.

From there I went by train to North Allerton, where I would spend the next 6 months in the orthopaedic department of the hospital, that was manned by mainly Ex South African orthopods. Each of the housemen had a mentor and worked under one of the orthopods. With stepping into the job I was told I should forget everything I'd learnt in South Africa and to start everything afresh. (Almost like the Gymnasium – "Here you were a rogue and a rogue was lower than crayfish shit, which is lower than sea level". At age 53 I thought that was a bit rough.)

I consulted the hospital psychologist to overcome my perceptions, but he was underqualified and I decided to just use him as a sounding board to gain my own insights on how to withstand this new assault.

To enable me to visit my english lady over weekends, when not on duty, she suggested that I could borrow money from her to buy a second-hand car. I went to see her until she started objecting. I was like a "Jack in the box" that she wanted to keep in a cupboard, only to be taken out when she was bored. She also had the fantasy that I was her toy boy as she was about 8 years older than me. She told me to make other friends. Due to my own self-hypnosis sessions, I discovered that she was exactly what I was trying to get away from – "Blame, Shame and Guilt" which is a form of abuse and it was also what I experienced as a houseman. On discussing this with the psychologist he saw himself as the "Deus ex Machina" and spilled all the beans of what

I had told him to the hospital psychiatrist, who was my mentor and he organised that I work under one of the other orthopods, which suited me just fine. (But it wasn't what I'd set out to accomplish and certainly not the way I wanted things to happen.)

At the end of the year I decided to break off my relationship with my English lady and promised to keep up the repayments for my car. I came across a Mensa dating advert where you basically set out your needs and personality on a data base questionnaire that then got matched to the data base of someone else of the opposite gender.

I received three replies and one matched all the criteria bar one. We made an arrangement to meet at the York theatre in January 1997. I had met my future wife, we got engaged 6 weeks later on Valentine's day and married in September of the same year, after I'd met her parents in Birmingham.

Around this time the first girlfriend claimed all the money back for the car I bought on her loan. My new mate was fortunately understanding and lent me the money to get rid of my obligations to her. (It was as if she thought she had bought me for the price of an old second-hand car, by then halfway paid back).

My last stint at NHS contracts before I started hospital locum work was at Gateshead hospital where my future wife joined me in the doctor's quarters.

This was where I learned what "cadaws" were. Every 2nd patient got their fingers trapped in "cadaws" until I asked one of them what exactly a "cadaw" is, so she said "ca daw, ca daw, the daw of a ca" Then a light bulb went up and I said "Oh, carrr doorrr". I also learned that ground is a floor and you greet by saying "hi ye".

My future wife and I travelled to South Africa several times to get my affairs sorted out. The first time in April to get my divorce papers translated to English and certified, and for my fiancé to meet my children. My boat was now already back at the factory and all my tools that were stored in a garage of my ex's friend, were taken to my storage location close to the airport for later shipping. Several items got lost.

We married on the 19th September, after fulfilling all my financial obligations to my ex-wife, with our daughters as witnesses. It was my daughter's first visit to England, to housesit in York, while we were on honeymoon.

The marriage went without a hitch. We had an old vintage bride's car for her journey to the hotel in York, where we were married, had the reception and then gathered in the bar area.

During the marriage ceremony we exchanged our vows to each other quoting alternative lines from the poem by Larry S. Chengges "I will always"

E.g. I will always promise to give you
the best of myself ...
and to ask you
no more than you can give.

I will always accept you the way you are ...
I fell in love with you
For the qualities, abilities,
And the outlook on life that you have,
And I won't try to reshape you
In a different image.
Etc. 7 verses in all.

****

For our honeymoon we sailed with a flotilla in the South Ionian, in a 27ft double keel sailing yacht.

Every morning we were briefed for the day's agenda, the weather and all the do's and don'ts – some days the briefing was for that day. On other days the briefing was for more than one day if the weather forecast was unfavourable. The activities entailed sailing from harbour to harbour on the same island or to different islands. We started off at Sivota harbour in Levkas island on day one it was, towards Kioni on Ithaca island.

The boat had a depth sounder and a log meter. I had my own mini-GPS. I recorded the times of direction changes and took waypoints at each tack, so that I could transfer my co-ordinates onto the chart.

In this way I knew where I was on the chart. In the middle of the island's coastline we had to look out for 3 wind mills, but I worked out our directions and co-ordinates and reached Kioni, without ever seeing the wind mills. The problem was that we sailed against the wind and depending which leg was close to the coastline you could either see the wind mills or miss them. One of the other boats changed direction and unknowingly sailed back to the same island from where we had come from, around the corner of Levkas island, instead of sailing to the Ithaca island. When he made radio contact to find out where we all were, we gathered he was still on Levkas, not at Vasiliki, the next port and it was too late to direct him to where we were and he had to stay put. He had to join another flotilla and while the time with them for meals and socialising until we arrived back at Vasiliki on our way back.

While underway we had to look out for the passenger ferries, which moved at far greater speeds than ourselves and sail over power right of way didn't apply which resulted in sailing in an unplanned direction, which was possibly one of the reasons our fellow partaker got lost.

In Kioni on Ithaca island, we were woken due to the thumping of the boat onto the harbour wall. We realised we were dragging our anchor from not having enough scope on the chain. I started blowing up our dinghy to put the anchor down further out, while my wife held the boat off the harbour wall but luckily an early fisherman came to our rescue and dropped the anchor further out in the bay.

After our disturbed night we sailed to Vathi on day 3, still on Ithaca island. In Vathi harbour, after we had moored, we saw a small fishing boat with a passenger ferry boat headed in its direction, we saw the fisherman frantically trying to start his engine without success – that was when he changed tack and frantically started rowing to get out of the ferry's way to our entertainment. (On one of the other boats there was a couple that told my wife, you could see ripples on the water if you reach climax, which almost ruined my honeymoon.) We later gathered that his wife had actually became pregnant during their sailing trip.

From Vathi bay we went past Kioni to Fiscardo on Cephalonia island on day 5. Here we saw how the other half lived when a luxury motor yacht moored as well.

On the 6th day we sailed back to Levkas island to Vasilico bay, where our lost participant was patiently waiting for us, completely rested out.

On day 7 we went to Nidri, where we saw a car with "Off with the goolies" painted on its bonnet. Here we watched para-sailing behind a motorboat, did some sun bathing and swimming.

We then escaped to Nikiana for a bit of private honeymoon on our own on day 9.

On day 10 we sailed on our own from Nikiana to Port Atheni on Meganissi island to rejoin the flotilla. Here some danced on the tables in Greek fashion. Most of them falling off. It was a great night, with plenty of laughter.

The next day there would be a regatta with a race around Onassis island and back to Port Vathi on Meganissi island. We came 2nd, but should have been 1st if my objection to a starboard rule had held sway.

On day 12 to Spartahori, still on Meganissi island, where we went with another couple up the hill to see how the locals lived in the village. All along the way there were shrines on the roadside, where someone local must have died. Some old, others new and some quite elaborate and attractive. Our women folk played cards with a couple of Greek men. You barely saw any Greek woman outside and when you saw them they were all dressed in black and quickly disappeared. We had some Greek cuisine at one of the café's.

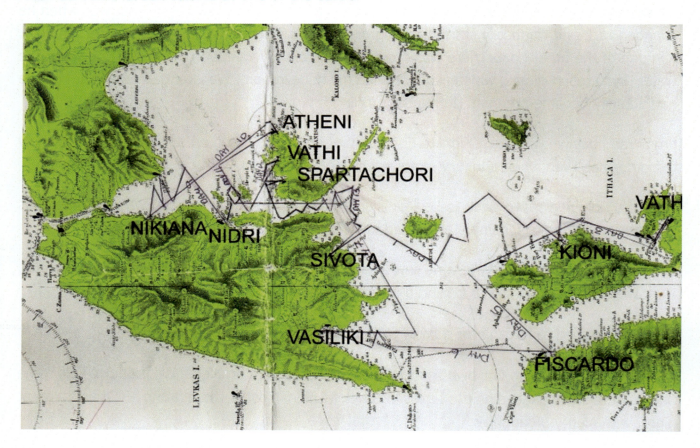

The next morning was our farewell to the other participants, exchange of addresses and telephone numbers, thanksgiving and humorous summaries and prize giving by the flotilla organisers. With our last briefing we departed to our final destination at Sivota on Levkas island, from where we would get transport back to the airport to fly back to England.

In March 1998 I went to South Africa to show it to my new wife. It was still like old South Africa and we hired a car, went to Sun City, visited my younger brother in Roodepoort and organised to see all my brothers, barring the one that had gone to America. It was the last time that we managed to meet up, as two of my younger brothers have since died. They both died of cancer and shared the same woman in succession.

Then we went to Kruger National Park, via Phalaborwa to enter the Park on its northern side We bought fruit along the road at a fraction of what it cost in the UK.

In the Park it was quite hot, but the hire car had air-conditioning and due to the fact that my wife was a bird watcher and was watching for movements rather than to spot animals, we soon saw lions missed by everyone else.

Back in Johannesburg after a night at my brother's we were on our way to Kimberley, 500 km distant, and the next morning to the Karoo National Park, 300km distant, for 2 days. On the way there we saw birds of prey, sitting on top of the telegraph poles, while we sped along at 80 mph. My wife exclaimed OMG when she saw the numbers of birds of prey there was in her Roberts bird book.

The next stop was George and Knysna, 500km from the park. At George my wife had the opportunity to get in a cage with a tame(ish) cheetah. She unfortunately had to take her glasses off, but she could stroke the cheetah half blind. One of the other women developed the desire to pull on the cheetah's tail and he warned everyone he was still a wild animal, by a big growl and snarling, exposing his teeth. The guard was not pleased and warned everyone off. We also saw Crocodiles being fed by a guard who was walking in between them.

From here we went to Knysna for 2 days and then to Somerset west 450 km South, where my daughter was living.

I arranged to get my yacht, "Green Dolphin", to the next stage of completion and then shipped to England. At my safe storage I also organised for the shipping of all my tools and books to be sent to the UK.

I showed my wife my little place in Mountain View. She now had a good idea of South Africa and how spread out it was.

With so much to see and to show there wasn't one moment of boredom. A large proportion of my holiday was paid for with my heaped up annuity, that remained behind in South Africa.

During this holiday South Africa was still tame and the folk still treated us with respect, unlike later years.

In between everything else I also made use of my time to visit my South African dentist. By being reliant on locum work meant that the month I had been in South Africa, I would have been without income in the UK and so I had to pay for a part of my holiday from my reserve. At this stage my mine company pension went towards the education of my two sons in information technology. They both opted for the same course and I was assured they would have future employment.

GIBRALTAR AND OTHER HOLIDAYS

With my sailing yacht in mind, I already had started doing sailing courses in Cape Town. My first course was competent yacht crew, although most of my experience was limited to dinghies. After my retirement from the mine company I did a course for "Yacht master" but without the practical examination, as I did not have the required number of hours in sailing experience.

During my honeymoon I met another sailing enthusiast with his own yacht, who planned to sail his boat from Hamble to Gibraltar to station his boat there. I asked if he would let me know when it would be, so that I could join him for the journey and aboard "Lady of the Hamble" to Falmouth, from where we would cross the channel on our way to Gibraltar.

Lady of the Hamble was a 40ft steel boat with a double bilge keel. It was a heavy displacement motor sailboat, with a massive diesel engine and large diesel tanks and a much smaller water tank. To compensate for the small water tank, there was a small one-cylinder engine with a water maker (desalinator). The sails were old and past best by date.

I took my own hand navigation GPS and small radio multiband receiver for weather information and the minimum of clothes. The time needed was 4 weeks. After an evening of jollity, we left the next morning – Him, a mate of his and myself. Thus a crew of 3 on the boat.

The food victualling was done by our wives. And with much waving we left Humber mouth on the way to Falmouth, along the coast. It was a long way from his mooring place to the mouth and we had a good weather forecast. We entered the Solent, leaving the Isle of Wight to our port and went past the Needles, before we reached the open sea.

The boat didn't roll much as we were sailing downwind under power. He also had dampers to limit the roll. With a stomach full from the previous evening and the fluid in my stomach being sploshed around I was soon queasy, but without vomiting. I had to look at the horizon to maintain my dignity to overcome the queasiness.

His mate knew this part of the coast pretty well and I left the navigation to them. I, fortunately insisted that my wife see to it that I had plenty of Rye vita and dry biscuits and I could withstand the hunger. Not that I was actually hungry, but it gave my stomach a chance to settle.

After more than 12 hours sailing under power, we arrived in Falmouth. One of the advantages in UK is that in summer you had 14 hours of daylight, followed by a long dusk. We moored at the first and best place and disembarked onto land.

The next day we moved to our allocated mooring. We went into town and bought some provisions, such as blocks for the sails and navigation charts. They wanted to save on charts, so I bought my own to supplement the navigation books I already had.

By this time the wind turned against us and we had to wait for 3 days before the wind was favourable again.

Eventually we left and took an East South East direction early that morning. The sea currents in the channel are quite strong and at one stage you would get pushed northwards and when the current turned, southwards again. As long as you kept on progressing eastwards, you would reach land on the other side. (Almost like the directions to the Caribbean islands – "You keep on moving south until the butter in the fridge melt and then you turn right in a western direction until you reach the islands".)

As navigator you are never lost, you just become unsure of your present position. I had my handheld GPS to determine where we were. The boat had an electronic GPS chart and what

I didn't understand then and don't understand even now, was why he was so hesitant to use it. He wanted to save on battery power. (With the engine running that shouldn't have been a problem, unless the batteries were shot and was of such a low capacity that it would have been a problem – normally you would have a separate engine starting battery, with domestic batteries for the rest.) We planned to sail overnight.

I was off watch and could go to bed, but he had a loose water pipe on deck that he wanted to use to hold the sails with, like a spinnaker pole. The pipe went roll, roll, roll, clunk as the boat was travelling along. With the help of self-hypnosis I managed to sleep using the noise as part of my mantra, instead of fighting it.

Early the next morning I was up and about and it wasn't long before first light. I was just in time to hear how they identified the "morning star" as either a ship's light or a light tower. We were to reach land by that evening. The channel was remarkably busy with shipping, but less so than at the Southern end of the channel, but you still had to be on your guard. The boat didn't have radar.

Late afternoon we arrived at "Lisigny Sur Mer", Brittany. We knew, as it was on the notice boards. We just had to determine where on the chart that was. As the tide between Jersey and Cherbourg would be against us, we decided to moor in the harbour and this was where my navigation books came into play. We tied up to the fishing boat mooring until the harbour master told us to move somewhere else.

It was the first time ever that I made a landfall in a foreign country by boat and the first time I set my eyes on the European coast. After payment for the mooring for the night we left early the next morning at low water – there were two channels out of the harbour, but we landed up in the dinghy channel and "boom", we grounded the boat and there we sat. "Lady of the Hamble" set foot on land before we did.

The tide was fortunately rising and shortly afterwards we floated again and could retrace our steps to the correct channel. The race of Alderney was a speed tide and rose by 13 meters between Cherbourg and Jersey.

We reached the Race with time to spare and sailed past Guernsey to Brittany and Le Brest small boat harbour where we could moor on the guest float. I could now go on land and walk on European soil. There was a boat chandler, a bar and a basic grocery store.

The weather forecast was against us again so we had to wait here for 3 to 4 days before we could go any further. This gave me time to explore the area on foot. The nearest town was 3 miles distant and you could see what the houses looked like – steep high rooves and detached houses with space in between, similar to what I was used to seeing in SA. Not the terrace dwellings and semi-detached house as in UK.

They were mostly painted white with the dark steep rooves. The area was beautifully green as most places along the coast. There was a military base nearby with a fair amount of activity.

After our boat owner irritated the local inhabitants for 4 days with his football stories and boasting to everyone how good the England team was, we eventually left for Spain, crossing the Bay of Biscay.

Now there was no wind at all and the master decided to test out his water-maker as the water tank was empty as he didn't fill it up at Le Brest. He unfortunately did not have a separate diesel supply and had to disconnect the fuel supply from the tank to the engine before he could start the small engine of the water-maker. The engine piping now unfortunately had a vacuum in it and it took 3 hours of wallowing in the middle of the Bay to resolve the problem and get the main engine going again.

I took command of the sails with the little bit of wind there was, to slowly make progress while we waited for the engine to get going.

We arrived at La Coruna at sunset, where we anchored outside the harbour to save money, but without any means to get on land. The next morning, we moved to the yacht club, so that we could disembark at will.

I got the task to buy the food. With my list I set off to a supermarket and battled to get hold of everything as labelling was marked in Spanish. Eventually I got someone to help me as the store was about to close and they wanted to go off for a siesta. With hand gestures and them guessing, I could get what I wanted, but it wasn't easy.

After 2 days of rest we sailed around the northern corner of Spain into the Atlantic coastal area to Vila Garcia. The Spanish architecture was pretty and impressive, old churches and buildings, open city plains and statues everywhere. The people were friendly, but everyone was going their own way. There were a great deal of open air cafeterias where you could have coffee or an ice cream.

Here we made friends with the owners of a group of boats, who were all on their way to Gibraltar or further on. We waited for them until they were ready to sail. This was where I bought an ordinarily cell phone, so I could talk to my new wife.

As a group we eventually departed for Gibraltar, but some wanted to go to Portugal first. I had my proper sea legs by now and was anxious to get to Gibraltar, so that I could get home – nice wasn't nice anymore. The next stop was Cadiz where we spent the night, and waited for the tide to turn before we went through the strait of Gibraltar to reach Gibraltar itself.

Our boat owner was so afraid that he would tear his sails, that he allowed the sails to flap into oblivion.

He continually waited for the right weather and with a single exception after waiting ended up in worse weather. Moral of the story – don't ever sail on a time schedule. It is not easy to judge a weather window – it does open up but it closes up just as easily.

In Gibraltar we had to wait for our respective flights back to UK, but I got my passport back, which he held me captive with. At long last I was back at home, several weeks later than planned, where my tools and books were waiting for me. All my books were there, but half of my tools, that were worth anything had been stolen by the company that shipped my possessions. They picked what they wanted and you can guess what the company was called. This was my first experience of the new South Africa. (The "have nots" who appointed themselves to take from the "haves" whatever they wanted.)

Now I could add a whole lot of hours and night sailing to my sailing log book for my "Yacht Master" certificate. The main thing I learned was to stay away from a water maker. I now had my own approach to sailing and how to plan my own boat for the future.

I eventually did launch my boat and did sail her for a couple of weekends, but my wife was not keen to actively go sailing and after all the delay with trying to get it CE certified and dealing with some rogue dealers in doing the same, I started seeing the light. I realised how the whole small craft recreation vessel industry worked and how the insurance and Marina businesses exploited boat owners, so I decided to sell at any price. I could recoup my losses, from the money I would have paid on insurance and marina fees, in no time. As it happened my health had started playing up and I had my gallbladder removed and with cardiac and lung complaints my fate would have been sealed, if I kept my dream.

1999 S-AFRICA VISITS AND THEREAFTER

My visits to South Africa were meant to familiarise my new wife with South Africa and to reaffirm my contact with my children. I ended up not succeeding in the latter because they had got so entrenched in their own lives. I honoured all my obligations and supported my daughter and one son with their weddings.

With my adopted son we told him from a young age he was adopted and he still recognised me as his Daddy. I helped him to identify his biological father (Who died from prostate cancer) and his biological family, none of whom were open to meet him. As a consolation I could inform him that his father's cousin's daughter is a prominent celebrity in Europe.

In 2015 we went to South Africa for the last time to the wedding of my adopted son. I contributed substantially to his wedding costs. South Africa has lost its charm for me and I could not bear to see it degrading into chaos and decline.

RETROSPECTION

My whole life I was judged to be negative and had to prove myself over and over again. (I was always on the defensive)

My first love disappointment was when I was in Std. VI and my childhood sweetheart got herself pregnant with someone much older at age 13 yrs. She never knew how I felt about her or at least I never told her.

I could view her as the first betrayal.

My second love disappointment was the girl I'd met in my second year medicine. During a temporarily breakup she got herself pregnant with a stranger in a one-night stand, whom she had to marry. The second betrayal.

I wasn't a good lover – I only learned to be a lover after I got divorced, but got into the same trap again but I could recognise it. (Blame, shame, guilt.) With my hypnotherapy I could help myself and became <u>positive</u> for the first time in my life. I knew who I was and what I wanted.

I have written this biography, partly to explain and illustrate to anyone that knew me in the old South Africa why I have been so "fucked up" and why I needed compensation in an all out exploitation of interests outside my marriage. I was "reborn" just before I left South Africa and to my frustration nobody that knew me previously even noticed that I've changed, with a few exceptions. They still wanted to blame and shame me and make me feel guilty. The abuse continued.

I wanted to finish all the unfinished business before I die – not that it would help me, but it may just help someone else to seek professional help from an experienced PhD qualified psychologist.

Betrayal and abuse is not on.

The keywords are trust, integrity and honesty. With that comes love, respect and peace.

Get rid of all the "...isms" and doctrines in your life.)

Gallery of Artistry.
<u>The Quest.</u>
<u>Peter Boshoff</u>

When I was small
I demanded love
And got love.

When I was young
I demanded love
And got conditional love.

Then I became older
And still wanted love
But there was none

Then I learned
To become a child again
And the love returned.

Dedication: To my dearest Heather.

At last I met my present wife and was married within a year and 24 years later we are still married, only 3 years short of my first marriage's duration.

My eldest two children visited me in England at my present address.

I believe in individual spiritualism (Not calling up ghosts) and very few people that know me know what that means unless they could spend some time with me and have been open to other philosophies than their own.

Basically that everyone knows themselves what is right or wrong if they listen to their own inner wisdom, without the input of religion or laws. "Religions are for those who are afraid of going to hell, Spiritualism are for those who already have been there!"

I am now happy and resigned to my own life and to hand over the reins to the next generation and I am wishing them well.

Farewell and may someone else learn from my mistakes.

("Don't worry, be happy.")

Printed in the United States
by Baker & Taylor Publisher Services